Gorgeous
Knitted Afghans

33 Great Designs for Creative Knitters

**Fatema, Khadija, and Hajera
Habibur-Rahman**

LARK BOOKS

A Division of Sterling Publishing Co., Inc.
New York

Editors
Marcianne Miller
Jane LaFerla

Art Director
Stacey Budge

Photographer
Stewart O'Shields

Cover Designer
Barbara Zaretsky

Illustrator
Orrin Lundgren

Associate Art Director
Shannon Yokeley

Art Intern
Melanie Cooper

Editorial Assistance
Delores Gosnel

Dedication

To our dearly loved mother and father, our loved brother Mustofa, our family and friends, and to all knitters whose dedication and ingenuity has brought the art of knitting alive.

Library of Congress Cataloging-in-Publication Data

Habibur-Rahman, Fatema.
  Gorgeous knitted afghans : 33 great designs for creative knitters /
Fatema, Khajida, and Hajera Habibur-Rahman.-- 1st ed.
      p. cm.
  Includes index.
  ISBN 1-57990-353-3 (hard cover)
  1. Knitting--Patterns. 2. Afghans (Coverlets) I. Habibur-Rahman,
Khajida. II. Habibur-Rahman, Hajera. III. Title.
  TT825.H256 2004
  746.43'0437--dc22
                                        2004009080

10 9 8 7 6 5 4 3 2 1

First Edition

Published by Lark Books, a division of
Sterling Publishing Co., Inc.
387 Park Avenue South, New York, N.Y. 10016

© 2004, Fatema Habibur-Rahman, Khajida Habibur-Rahman, Hajera Habibur-Rahman

Distributed in Canada by Sterling Publishing,
c/o Canadian Manda Group, One Atlantic Ave., Suite 105
Toronto, Ontario, Canada M6K 3E7

Distributed in the U.K. by Guild of Master Craftsman Publications Ltd., Castle Place, 166 High Street,
Lewes, East Sussex, England
BN7 1XU
Tel: (+ 44) 1273 477374, Fax: (+ 44) 1273 478606, Email: pubs@thegmcgroup.com, Web:
www.gmcpublications.com

Distributed in Australia by Capricorn Link (Australia) Pty Ltd.,
P.O. Box 704, Windsor, NSW 2756 Australia

Every effort has been made to ensure that all the information in this book is accurate. However, due to differing conditions, tools, and individual skills, the publisher cannot be responsible for any injuries, losses, and other damages that may result from the use of the information in this book.

If you have questions or comments about this book, please contact:
Lark Books
67 Broadway
Asheville, NC 28801
(828) 253-0467
Printed in China

ISBN 1-57990-353-3

table of contents

introduction

WE THREE SISTERS WERE brought up in a home decorated with exquisite Islamic art, handmade Persian and Turkish rugs, and Indian embroidered pillows. We come from a family rich in heritage, where several different languages are spoken. Our father is from West Bengal, India, a region known for the arts. Our mother's lineage is a mixture of Afghani, Bengali, Uzbek, Mongolian, Punjabi (Pakistan), and Yemeni descent. It is from this fortunate mix of cultures, each known for their beautiful patterned textiles, exuberant use of color, and attention to craftsmanship, that we were inspired to write this book.

We have created the 33 afghans in this book to share a part of our tradition with you. *Modern Reflections* on page 145 incorporates embroidered mirrors and paisley, *Bold Heritage* on page 59 uses duplicate stitch to present patterned motifs, and *Fiesta* on page 67 reminds us of some of the colorful, open-air markets that we've seen in our travels.

Usually afghans are made with basic colors and stitches, but we wanted to bring to you a variety of designs using a sampling of some of the luscious yarns available today. Every effort was put into creating afghans that knitters on all skill levels—from beginner to experienced—could complete. We have provided clear instructions and easy-to-read charts with legends that will lead you through the patterns.

From the age of five, we were taught to knit basic stitches, embroider samples, and crochet the chain stitch. Our mother, a college graduate, believed all ladies must learn the domestic arts—from knitting to sewing, embroidery to cooking—as her mother did before her, and she patiently guided our progress. After mastering a little of all the arts, we ventured out on our own with our knitting, mixing influences from our Eastern art with a range of western classical and contemporary styles.

After spending more than a decade designing afghans, we wanted to present them as works of art. Beyond their function as blankets or throws, we see them as canvases waiting for the perfect combination of stitches and yarns. We've enjoyed creating patterns that we think fit a range of decors—from a contemporary urban living room to a wood-paneled retreat glowing with firelight.

While these afghans can be used in almost any setting, we want you to also consider their value as heirlooms-in-the-making—as a wonderful way to preserve your own family's heritage.

We believe that a person's art is a reflection of their inner soul. We hope you enjoy making these afghans as much as we have, and that you use our designs to expand your own skills and creativity.

Fatema, Khadija & Hajera

the basics

Materials, Tools & Techniques

Yarn

Yarn falls into three fiber categories: animal (e.g., wool, mohair, cashmere, silk), vegetable (e.g., cotton, linen, ramie), and synthetic (e.g., acrylic, rayon, polyester). Each type of yarn needs its own special care, and the afghan may either need to be hand washed, machine washed, or dry cleaned. Make sure you check the label for the yarn's care instructions since it will help ensure that your afghan stays beautiful and lasts longer.

YARN WEIGHTS

When you hear talk about yarn weights, it's common to immediately think about the weight of each skein; however, knitters are speaking about the thickness of the yarn strand. At the local yarn store, you will notice many yarns ranging from Superfine (thinnest) to Super Bulky (thickest); either way, the yarn weight is important when determining how many skeins or balls you'll need for a pattern's recommended gauge and needle size.

Yarn weight is divided into six categories: Superfine (sock, fingering), Fine (sport, baby), Light (double knitting, light worsted), Medium (worsted), Chunky (craft), and Super Bulky (bulky). It's important to note that you should match the weight of the yarns specified in your pattern with the substituted yarn of your choice.

DYE LOTS

When you purchase your yarn, you'll notice a dye lot number. Yarns with the same number are ones that were dyed at the same time in the same dye vat. If you buy yarns with different dye lot numbers, you are buying the same color but run the risk of getting yarn that is a slightly different shade. Therefore, it's important to

Ply

Ply refers to the number of strands that make up the yarn's thread. A single ply is one strand of spun yarn. Yarns can be two-ply, three-ply, four-ply, or more. Plying makes yarn stronger and more uniform in diameter.

purchase enough yarn with identical dye lot numbers to produce an afghan in the same shade. If you're worried about initially buying too much yarn, keep your receipts since many stores will accept unused yarns.

BALLS, SKEINS, HANKS, OR CONES

When you purchase your yarn, you'll notice that it comes wrapped in different shapes, such as balls, skeins, hanks, or cones. The same yarn can come in several shapes, but you'll find that cones hold more yardage. Hanks need to be wound in a ball prior to use—you can use your hands or a ball winder, found at any knitting store. Be careful to wind the yarn loosely; if you wind the yarn too tightly the yarn might loose its resilience. Some knitters prefer to purchase their yarn in cones for large projects. Working with cones keeps all the yarn in one place—and keeps you from searching for a lost ball of yarn.

Yarn Storage

It's very important to keep your yarn stored in a clean place, especially white yarn. To keep the yarn from becoming discolored, you should not store it in direct sunlight. When we knit, we keep the yarn in a plastic bag and pull from it when needed—this keeps the yarn off the floor and protects it from dust.

YARN SUBSTITUTION

We recommend you use the yarns listed in the pattern to achieve satisfactory results. However, by the time you go to purchase the yarn, there may be some that are discontinued or unavailable in your local store. In other cases, you may be allergic to wool and prefer using acrylic when knitting. You should try substituting yarns. Just keep in mind that when you decide to substitute, you should knit a gauge sample and check its compatibility with the pattern's requirement. Your sample must be consistent with the pattern—if your gauge sample is larger than the requirements, use smaller needles; or if the gauge sample is smaller, use larger needles.

GAUGE

Gauge is the number of rows and stitches in an inch. To measure the gauge, you use a measuring tape or gauge tool to compare the knits' measurement to the pattern's required gauge. This lets you know whether the needles and yarn you're using are compatible with the particular pattern. It is important that you have the right gauge before you work, since your afghan may end up a size too big or too small.

An "engauging" story: When one of us, we'll name her "Pity," began to knit, she did not take gauge into consideration. Instead of checking her gauge, Pity began knitting a sweater with the wrong needle and yarn type. She substituted a 6 needle with an 8, and used worsted-weight acrylic yarn instead of light cotton yarn. She ended up with a large sweater that stretched down to her knees instead of to her waist. It was a pitiful sight with hard work gone to waste, but it was a valuable lesson. From then on, she always knitted a swatch and checked the gauge before starting any project.

Checking the Gauge

Checking the gauge is easy. After making a sample you measure it, then you compare your sample's measurements to the pattern's required gauge. You can make any needed adjustments by changing the needle size.

1. Count the number of stitches across 2"/5cm. Multiply it by 2 and you will get the number of stitches for 4"/10cm as shown in figure 1.
2. Count the number of rows in 2"/5cm. Multiply it by 2 and you will get the number of rows per 4"/10cm as shown in figure 2.

fig. 1

fig. 2

Tools

When you stroll through the knitting aisle, you'll notice a large assortment of knitting tools and accessories. We find that they make our knitting easier and allow us to explore a wide variety of designs and techniques. You might question which ones are essential for knitting the afghan. The tools listed below come in handy when it's time to create cables, mark stitches, change colors, and weave ends.

KNITTING NEEDLES

What would we do without them! They come in a variety of sizes, materials, and shapes. We call them kneedles (ka•nēd´•ls) to distinguish them from our sewing and embroidery needles. Using wooden knitting needles is encouraged for the first-time knitter, or when you're using slippery yarn, since the stitches do not easily slide off them. Knitters suffering from arthritis will find bamboo needles wonderful to use because they warm up when your knitting. Plastic needles are perfect for knitting quietly and quickly. Metal needles, such as the nickel-plated ones, accommodate fast knitters who have stacks of projects waiting to be completed.

Circular, Single- and Double-Pointed Needles. We usually use circular needles in knitting afghans since there many stitches to knit and hold. You treat circular needles just like straight needles by knitting to the end of the row and turning the needle around to knit on the wrong side. When you purchase your circular needles, you will notice that the flexible plastic cord is twisted no matter how much you pull and stretch it, but there's a way to straighten this out. Dip your needles into warm, soapy water for a few minutes, then lay the needles straight until dry. Voilà, you have new circular "straight" needles. If you want them back in their original shape, well, we'll just let you figure that one out. You'll find that single-pointed straight needles (pointed on one end) or double-pointed needles (pointed on each end) are handy for knitting small pieces.

Cable Needles. We have many different shapes and sizes of cable needles in our knitting supplies—some look like safety pins while others resemble fishhooks—but you will find that they all provide the same results. Choose cable needles according to your need and the size of the cables. Packaged cable needles are available in all cable sizes.

STITCH MARKERS

In knitting you may often forget which stitch you are on. Stitch markers help you remember where to start shaping or begin a new stitch pattern. Like cable needles, stitch markers come in different sizes and colors. You will notice in some of the patterns that stitch markers are used to separate the border stitches from the patterns. When knitting stitches, place a marker (pm), then slip the marker onto the right needle once you reach it.

YARN BOBBINS

Yarn bobbins, designed to hold small amounts of yarn, are used when the pattern calls for several colors. You can purchase yarn bobbins or make your own from cardboard. When using yarn bobbins, you simply wind the yarn around the bobbin and work from that yarn when the pattern calls for a color change. You want to be sure to keep the bobbins separate from each other to prevent the yarns from tangling and to minimize your frustration.

POINT PROTECTORS

Point protectors keep your needle points covered when not in use to protect children and others from injury. If you knit with small children in the house, it's important that you have them on hand. There may be times when you think your needle is safely tucked into your bag, but later realize that it's poking through.

ROW COUNTERS

Sometimes we tend to rely on our memory, but end up forgetting the

row we're working on, particularly after returning to a project several days later. Row counters are necessary when you need to keep track of your rows. You slide the row counter onto the end of your needle, and every time you complete a row you just turn the knob.

TAPESTRY NEEDLES

Tapestry needles, distinguished by their large eyes, are practical tools for seaming ends, creating a duplicate stitch, working various embroidery stitches on the afghans, and weaving in ends.

CROCHET HOOKS

We use a large crochet hook for attaching the fringes and tassels to the afghans. They are also used for creating crocheted borders on some of the patterns.

How to Make a Yarn Bobbin

1. Using a strong piece of cardboard, draw and cut out a bobbin pattern, as shown in figure 3.
2. Wrap the yarn around the bobbin until it is full, as shown in figure 4.

fig. 3

fig. 4

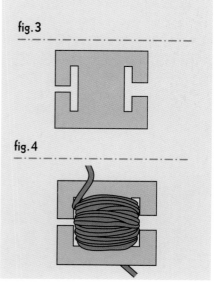

TAPE MEASURE

A tape measure is essential for measuring the stitches and rows of your gauge and the size of your afghan during knitting, blocking, and finishing.

PINS

Look for long durable pins that will be sufficient for holding the afghan or pieces in place when blocking.

Knitting the Afghan

This part of the chapter will take you through all you need to know to knit the afghans in this book. You'll find descriptions of what you can expect to find in the instructions—including materials, pattern notes, special abbreviations, charts, and legends—as well as explanations of any special techniques that we used.

SKILL LEVEL

We have listed the skill level for each afghan to help you identify the patterns within your range of expertise—beginner, easy, intermediate, and experienced. However, you shouldn't be discouraged from making an afghan solely by the level listed. If you feel that you can accomplish an intermediate afghan, even though you consider yourself a beginner, then go ahead and try it out.

YARN AND MATERIALS

In this section of the instructions we have listed the yarn and tools needed to create the afghans. For the yarns, you'll see the total yardage/meters and type of yarn

used. Since some of the afghans require more than one type of yarn or color, we labeled each yarn with letters to help you distinguish which yarns are being used in the instructions. At the end of each instruction you will find the brand name and the number of skeins of yarns used in creating the afghan.

PATTERN NOTE

Here, you will find specific information that is unique to the pattern. These notes will help you follow the instructions to complete the afghan.

SPECIAL ABBREVIATIONS

Besides the known common abbreviations, this section of the instructions will include any special abbreviations that need to be explained before you begin to knit.

PATTERN STITCH

This section names and defines the stitch pattern. You'll be able to refer to it when instructed to do so.

AFGHAN

This is where you will find instructions that are specific to making the afgan.

CHARTS

Throughout this book you'll notice that the majority of the afghans are accompanied by a chart. Many knitters find it easy to knit with charts since it gives a visual representation of the stitches and shows the shaping of the pieces. Some of the charts in this book will show you where to change colors or attach knitted pieces. To make it easier for you to read the charts, we give you permission to enlarge them.

fig. 5

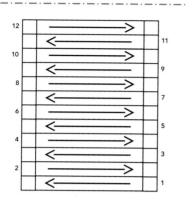

Beginning to knit on a RS row

fig. 6

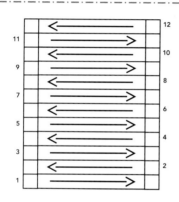

Beginning to knit on a WS row

fig. 7

Translates to:

Row 1 and all (WS): K1, p10, k1, *p3, k1, p10, k1 rep from * to end.

Row 2: *P1, k10, p1, yo, sk2p, yo; rep from * end p1, k10, p1.

Row 4: *P1, k1, [yo, k1] 3 times, [skp] 3 times, p1, yo, sk2p, yo; rep from *, end p1, k1, [yo, k1] 3 times, [skp] 3 times, p1.

Row 6: *P1, [k2tog] 3 times, [k1, yo] 3 times, k1, p1, yo, k3tog, yo; rep from *, end p1, [k2tog] 3 times, [k1, yo] 3 times, k1, p1.

When reading the chart, you will notice numbers on the left- and right- hand sides. The numbers on the right side refer to all the Right Side (RS) rows, while the numbers on the left side refer to all the Wrong Side (WS) rows. On other charts you will find that the numbering starts on the left. This means the first row is a WS row. When you begin knitting, you will read the row from right to left when working on a RS row, as shown in figure 5, and read the row from left to right when working on the WS row, as shown in figure 6. For example:

The charts have symbols indicating the stitches to use. Charts will have legends that translate any uncommon symbols specific to that pattern. A red outline on the chart shows that stitches need to be repeated. Figure 7 is an example of a chart followed by its translation to instructions. You will find a list of common abbreviations used in this book at the end of this chapter. The patterns will list any special abbreviations to be used in the design.

KNITTING WITH MULTIPLE STRANDS

Many of the afghans give instructions to knit with multiple strands, especially when working with thinner yarns. One way to make this easier is to join the yarns together and roll them into one ball prior to knitting. By doing this you will avoid tangled yarns and messy work.

BORDER STITCHES

You will find that many of the afghans in this book have border stitches knit either in garter (knit on both sides) or seed stitch. Using stitch markers will help you distinguish between the actual pattern and the beginning or end of border stitches.

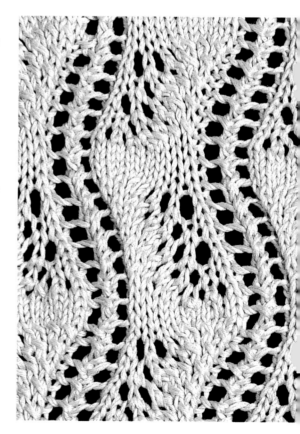

KNITTING WITH SEVERAL COLORS

Just as artists use paint and brushstrokes in their artwork, knitters use yarn as their palette and needles for brushes. You will notice in our afghans that we use many combinations of color to create a variety of shades or to produce dramatic effects. It's important to remember that when many color changes are needed, you should twist the yarns to prevent holes from forming in the work. For knitted pieces that require several color changes in a row, you will find it easier to use bobbins that will help you knit smoothly without worrying about tangles. The majority of the afghans use the technique of intarsia (see figures 8 and 9) that allows you to change colors without carrying a strand of yarn on the back of the work.

fig. 8

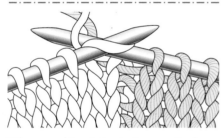

When working intarsia in a vertical line on the knit side, pick up the new color under the previous color.

fig. 9

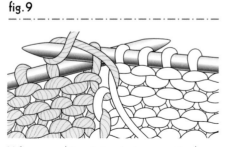

When working intarsia in a vertical line on the purl side, pick up the new color under the previous color.

USING BOBBLES

You can produce a three-dimensional effect on your afghan with easy-to-knit bobbles. Figures 10 and 11 show how to make a bobble.

fig. 10

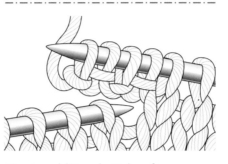

Create additional stitches from one stitch by knitting through the front loop and then through the back loop. Repeat in this manner until the number of stitches noted in the instructions is made. Then slip the worked stitch from the left needle.

fig. 11

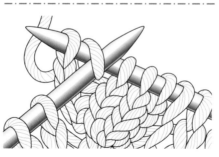

Using the left needle slip the second stitch over the first, then repeat for the remaining stitches made in figure 10, slipping them one at a time over the first stitch. The bobble has been made.

KNITTING WITH BEADS

Knitting with beads brings a special glow to your work. You can add beads by stitching them on by hand after you've completed your knitting, or you can knit with the beads by stringing them on the yarn before beginning to knit. We found that stringing the yarn with beads first saves more time than sewing them on later. Figure 12 shows how to thread beads, and figure 13 shows you how to knit with them.

fig. 12

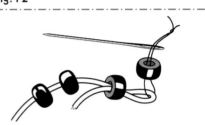

If you find it difficult to thread the yarn through the beads because either the yarn is too thick or the needle's eye is larger than the hole in the bead, you can use a thin sewing thread and needle to help you. First use them to make a loop around the yarn. Then insert the needle into the bead, pulling the thread and yarn through. String the remaining beads using the same technique.

fig. 13

Work the stitch as you normally would, pushing the bead over the right needle through the stitch on the left needle.

USING EMBROIDERY STITCHES

In this book, you will notice that we used quite a few embroidery stitches to decorate the afghans. Following are instructions for making them.

Chain Stitch (figure 14). This stitch is made by inserting the needle into a loop of thread and repeating to make a continuous chain.

Duplicate Stitch (figure 15). This stitch duplicates the look of multi-colored knitting by covering knit stitches with another yarn. The stitch is made by alternately inserting the needle into the top two loops of a stitch, then into the bottom two loops.

French Knot (figure 16). These embroidered knots add texture or can replicate floral forms. They are made by wrapping the thread around the needle, holding the thread tight, then reinserting the needle close to where it emerged.

Lazy Daisy Stitch (figure 17). The basis of this stitch is the simple chain stitch, but instead of making a continuous line, each loop is anchored at the top with a stitch. As its name implies, this stitch makes great flowers.

fig. 14

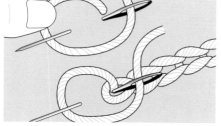

fig. 16

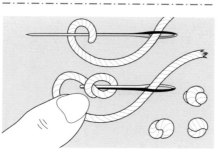

fig. 15

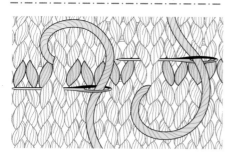

fig. 17

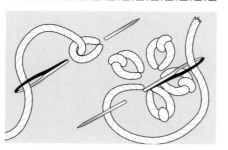

fig. 18

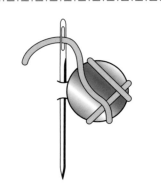

fig. 19

fig. 20

fig. 21

fig. 22

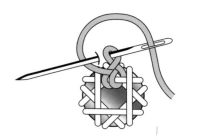

Shisha Stitch. Shisha is the Urdu/Hindi word for glass or mirror, and refers to the small mirrors and bits of glass that are embroidered on Indian textiles; the shisha stitch is used for attaching them. When you make the first foundation stitches, they need to be tight and slightly away from the edge of the shisha. Making the stitches loose or close to the edge will result in the shisha falling out.

1. Work the four foundation stitches as shown in figures 18 and 19.

2. Then repeat with four more stitches as shown in figure 20.

3. Bring the needle alongside the shisha's edge, passing it under the foundation stitches. With the yarn under the needle, make an even stitch over the edge of the mirror and, keeping the yarn under the needle, pull tight. See figure 21.

4. Keeping the yarn below the needle, pass it under the foundation stitches. When making the second stitch and similar stitches around the edge of the mirror, pull the needle through the loop made on the previous loop stitch. See figure 22.

MAKING MISTAKES

If you look closely at handmade carpets, you'll find slight mistakes in the pattern. This is usually the identifying mark that the carpet is indeed made by hand rather than a machine and is thus more valuable. Keeping this in mind, don't worry about any small mistakes you might make in your knitting—they are the marks of a handmade treasure.

COMPLETING THE AFGHAN

The old saying "a stitch in time saves nine," can best be put to use when knitting afghans. We have found that our projects take less time and cause us less frustration when we set aside a time to knit, even if it's in the late hours of the night and all we do is knit a few stitches or even a row. Knitting can be done almost anywhere; while waiting for the bus, at a busy clinic, during lunch hour, or in between classes. If you have the time, grab your needles and knit away.

Finishing

Once the major portion of your afghan is knitted, it's time to think about the finishing touches—seaming it together if it was made in separate pieces, blocking, adding tassels or fringes, and making a knit or crocheted border.

SEAMING

Many of the afghans in this book are knit in pieces, making them ideal projects for knitting outside the home. When it's time to attach the pieces, we prefer seaming them together on the right side using the invisible seam, otherwise known as the mattress stitch, as shown in figure 23. This method produces a clean seam for a natural look, as shown in figure 24.

fig. 23

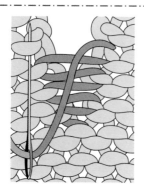

Place the two knitted pieces side by side, matching the rows and stitches. Begin by inserting the needle under the top loop on one side and bottom loop on the second piece.

fig. 24

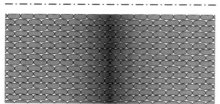

The final seam is nearly invisible.

BLOCKING

Blocking your afghan evens out the stitches and gives it a permanent shape. By following the manufacturer's instructions on the yarn label, you can avoid damage from using too much steam, water, or heat.

You don't need to purchase a blocking pad for afghans because it's more convenient to use a carpeted floor or bed for large pieces. However, in case the yarn should bleed when wet, you need to cover the carpet or bed before placing the afghan on top of it. When we block afghans, we place them on a carpet in the warmest area of our home. To prevent mildew, avoid blocking your afghan on humid days.

To begin blocking, first measure the afghan. The blocked afghan will match the pattern's measurements and you will shape it accordingly. When wet blocking the afghan, you can either spray it with water when it is pinned down (see figure 25), or you can dip the afghan in water, squeeze out the excess water until damp, then pin it down and allow it to dry naturally. Use pins to hold the edges as you define the shape. Be sure you don't overstretch or flatten any textured surfaces such as cables or bobbles.

For steam blocking (see figure 26), pin the afghan on the surface and set your iron to the correct fiber setting. Hold the iron several inches above the afghan and press the steam button over each area. If the iron is too close to the work it may flatten or disfigure the afghan. For delicate fibers, place a clean cloth, such as a bed sheet, over the afghan to prevent direct contact that can cause shrinking or scorching.

fig. 25

When wet blocking, the afghan is placed on a padded surface and pinned. You can use a spray bottle to spray water on the afghan, then allow it to air dry.

fig. 26

When steam blocking, hold the iron several inches above the afghan, and steam each area as you pass over it. Place a bed sheet over the afghan if there is a possibility that the afghan may get scorched.

TASSELS, FRINGE, AND POMPOMS

Adding tassels, fringe, and pompoms can add pizzazz to your afghan. Many of the patterns include them to complement the design.

Tassels

1. As instructed in the pattern, cut a cardboard strip to the required width. Wrap the yarn around the width of the cardboard the number of times indicated. Thread yarn through a tapestry needle and insert it through the top of the cardboard, capturing all yarns. Tie the top, leaving a long length of extra thread for encircling the head and for attaching the tassel. See figure 27.

2. Remove the tassel from the cardboard. Wrap some of the long length of thread around the top half for creating the head. Secure the thread, then insert the remaining length back and through the middle of the head. Trim the bottom edges. See figure 28.

fig.27

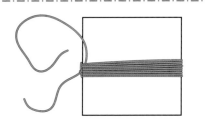

fig.28

fig.29

fig.30

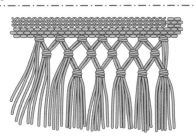

Fringe

As instructed in the pattern, cut a cardboard strip to the required width. For each fringe, wrap the yarn around the width of the cardboard the number of times indicated in the pattern. Cut the yarn free along one edge of the cardboard. Remove the yarn from the cardboard, and fold the strands in half. As shown in figure 29, use a large crochet hook to insert the strands through the back of the afghan, capturing the looped yarn. Pull through. Pull the yarn loop around the edge and draw the fringe tail inside of the loop. Pull the tail to tighten, and trim the bottom edges.

Knotted Fringe

Make fringe as shown in figure 29. Take half of the strands from one fringe and half of the strands from another and knot them together, as shown in figure 30. Repeat across and for the levels of knotting you desire.

Pompoms

1. Cut out two cardboard circles, each 4"/10 cm in diameter. Cut a pie-shaped wedge in the circles. Then cut out a circle approximately 1½"/3.8cm diameter from the middle of each circle, as shown in figure 31.

2. Holding the two circles together, wrap yarn around the cardboard. Carefully slip your scissors between the circles and cut along the edges, as shown in figure 32.

3. Cut a 10"/25.4 cm piece of yarn and slip it between the two circles, tying the pompom securely in the middle as shown in figure 33. Remove the cardboard and trim the edges of the pompom, keeping the long string intact.

fig.31

fig.32

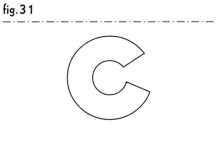

fig.33

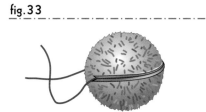

CROCHET EDGINGS

Some of the afghan patterns include crocheted edgings. The most common crochet stitches used were the chain stitch, slip stitch, single crochet, and double crochet.

Chain Stitch (ch). See figure 34. Begin with a slipknot. With the loop on hook, wrap yarn over the hook once and pull it through the loop. This is the foundation row for crochet.

Slip Stitch (sl st). See figure 35. Insert the hook through the next stitch keeping the previous loop on the hook. Wrap the yarn over the hook once and pull it through both loops on hook.

Single Crochet (sc). See figure 36. Insert the hook through the next stitch, keeping the previous loop on the hook. Wrap the yarn once over the hook and pull through the first stitch. Wrap the yarn over the hook once again and pull through both loops on the hook.

fig.34

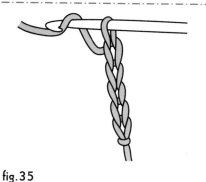

fig.35

fig.36

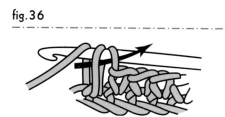

Double Crochet (dc)

1. Following figure 37, keep the previous loop on the hook, wrap the yarn once over the hook, and insert it through the fourth chain. Draw the yarn through the fourth chain, making three loops.

2. Wrap the yarn over the hook once and draw it through the first two loops on the hook, as shown in figure 38.

3. Wrap the yarn over the hook once again and draw it through the remaining two loops, as shown in figure 39.

4. Figure 40 shows an example of double crochet.

fig.37

fig.38

fig.39

fig.40

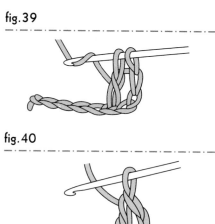

Caring for Your Afghan

Congratulations! You finally completed your afghan. Perhaps the first question that comes to mind is how do I keep my afghan looking as beautiful as it is now? The answer is in how you care for it.

WASHING

Acrylic and some treated wool yarns are machine washable, while other yarns need to be hand washed or dry-cleaned. It's important to follow the care instructions located on the yarn's label, otherwise your afghan can shrink or stretch during washing; the colors may bleed; or the afghan may even tear if it's made with delicate yarns. If you're unsure how to care for your afghan and want to be on the safe side, it's always best to hand wash it. If you decide to use any product with which you are unfamiliar, try it out on a yarn swatch before using it on your afghan. Another word of caution: handle your wet afghan gently to make sure it doesn't stretch out of shape.

DRYING

After taking special care when washing your afghan, you will need to take as much care when drying. To keep your afghan in shape, you should avoid wringing your afghans to remove excess water or hanging it on a clothesline. The safest way to dry the afghan is to place it on a flat surface to be air-dried. To prevent mildew, make sure it is in a well-ventilated room. There should be no direct sunlight on the afghan as it dries. The sun can bleach the afghan or make it shrink.

STORAGE

At some time it may be necessary for you to store your afghan, especially if you made it as an heirloom. One of wool's worst enemies is moth larvae that feed on wool. In order to keep your afghans safe, mothballs or cedar chips can help protect your afghans from these pests. Mothballs should not be placed directly on the afghan but wrapped in cheesecloth or cotton to minimize direct contact. If you have one, a cedar chest is the perfect place to store your afghan. Be sure to take your stored afghans out periodically to air them. When placing it back in storage, be sure to change the folds to prevent permanent creases from developing.

PETS

Some pet lovers may be hesitant to knit an afghan because they know their pets would get more enjoyment out of it than they would. There are a few options for preserving your work even though you may have a houseful of pets. One way is to hang it on your wall as you would a quilt. It's a beautiful way to decorate your home with vibrant colors and texture. Additionally, your family members and friends will compliment your creativity. Of course, you can always knit two afghans, one for yourself and a special washable one for your pampered pet.

KNITTING IN GROUPS

Knitting groups across America have become very popular in recent years. These groups are special since they link a variety of age groups and a diversity of people together to share knitting techniques and exchange ideas. Group members help and encourage each other to start and finish projects. In some groups, knitters work together to knit blankets for premature babies at their local hospital or knit socks for victims of war-torn countries. You can find a knitting group in your area by contacting your local yarn store or knitting guild, or by forming your own group with family and friends.

Afghan Abbreviations

beg beginning

beg pat beginning of pattern

BO bind off

CO cast on

cont continue, continuing

dec decrease

dk pat double-knit pattern

dk rec pat double-knit reverse pattern

dpn double-pointed needle(s)

dyo double yarn over

foll follow(s), following

g st garter stitch

inc increase

k knit

k1inc1 knit one, increase one

k2tog knit two together

k3tog knit three together

k tbl knit through back loop

LH left hand

LT left twist

M1 make one

MB make bobble

p purl

p1inc1 purl one, increase one

p2tog purl two together

p3tog purl three together

p tbl purl through back look

pat pattern

pm place marker

pnso pass next stitch over

psso pass slip stitch over

rem remain, remaining

rep repeat

RH right hand

RS right side

RT right twist

s1 slip one stitch knitwise if following stitch is a knit stitch, or slip purlwise if the following stitch is a purl stitch

sk2p slip one stitch knitwise, knit one stitch, knit another stitch, pass slipped stitch over both knit stitches (decrease from 3 stitches to 2 stitches)

skp slip one stitch knitwise, knit one stitch, pass slipped stitch over knit stitch (decrease from 2 stitches to 1 stitch)

spp slip one stitch purlwise, purl one stitch , pass slipped stitch over purl stitch (decrease from 2 stitches to 1 stitch)

sppp slip one stitch purlwise, purl one stitch, purl another stitch, pass slipped stitch over both purl stitches (decrease from 3 stitches to 2 stitches)

ssk slip one stitch knitwise, slip one stitch, knit through both slipped stitches (decrease from 2 stitches to 1 stitch

st stitch

sts stitches

st st stockinette stitch

tbl through the back loop

tog together

WS wrong side

wyib with yarn in back

wyif with yarn in front

yo yarn over

the projects

Throughout the ages, knitters have made colorful blankets for warmth. The blankets often incorporated design motifs unique to their culture of origin. Today these beautiful knitted blankets are known as afghans.

Typically the word Afghan, from the Persian language, refers to the people of Afghanistan. Now it commonly describes all crocheted or knitted throws and blankets. The origin of this usage is thought to have started with the British occupation of Afghanistan in the early 1800s. As the British exported Afghan textiles to their country, including knitted lap robes, rugs, and shawls, it's easy to see how the term afghan came into popular use.

The 33 gorgeous projects in this book will complement a variety of decors—from country house to city loft. Whether you make an afghan for your home, or as a gift for a new baby, a spouse, a parent, a son, or a daughter, you'll find that a handmade afghan is a true expression of love translated into a beautiful work of art.

mediterranean
watercolors

The lush colors used in this afghan are reminiscent of the rich and varied colors of the Mediterranean coast. The double knitting technique, which enhances the yarn colors, is a simple yet exquisite stitch that allows even a beginning knitter to finish the project in a few days.

Finished Measurements

42 x 52"/107 x 132cm, blocked

Yarn

Color A: Approx total: 489yd/447m wool, medium weight yarn

Color B: Approx total: 380yd/347m mohair/wool/nylon blend, medium weight yarn

Color C: Approx total: 280yd/256m cotton, medium weight tape

Color D: Approx total: 250yd/229m cotton/wool blend, bulky weight yarn

Color E: Approx total: 294yd/269m wool/viscose, medium weight yarn

Materials

Knitting needles: 8 mm (Size 11 U.S.) *or size to obtain gauge*

Tapestry needle for weaving the ends

Large crochet hook for attaching the fringe

Cardboard strip, 5"/12.7cm wide, for making the fringe

Gauge

14 sts = 4"/10cm over St st using A, B, D, E

16 sts = 4"/10cm over St st using C

Always take time to check your gauge.

Pattern Note

The pattern calls for a double wrap. To do this, you wrap the yarn twice around the needle instead of once when knitting the stitch. This will form two loops per st.

Pattern Stitch

MEDITERRANEAN WATERCOLOR STITCH (CHART A)

Preparation Row: K by wrapping yarn twice for each st. Total of 252 sts (126 pairs).

Row 1: K first loop of pair, leaving second loop of pair on needle. * K second loop of pair with first loop of next pair by wrapping yarn twice; rep from * to last loop, end by knitting last loop by double wrap.

Rep row 1 for pat.

Chart A

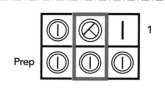

	Knit
$\boxed{\textcircled{\text{I}}}$	Knit by wrapping yarn twice
$\boxed{\otimes}$	Ktog second loop of pair with first loop of next pair by wrapping yarn twice

Afghan

With A, CO 126 stitches. Knit one row. Work the prep row once, * work the pattern for eight rows. Rep from * for B, C, D, E, A twice more. Bind off all stitches.

Finishing

Weave the ends in. Block lightly.

Fringe

The general instructions for making fringe are on page 20. Make enough fringes to attach across the two edges of the afghan. Using A, B, C, D, and E, wrap the yarn seven times around the width of the cardboard strip. Attach the colored fringes alternately along the edges of the afghan, then trim the ends of the fringes.

Design Tip

This afghan is great for using leftover yarns in an assortment of colors.

This afghan was knit with:

(A) 3 hanks of Colinette Yarns' *Skye*, 100% pure wool yarn, medium, worsted weight, 100g = approx 163yd/150m per hank, color #58 Renaissance

(B) 2 hanks of Colinette Yarns' *Mohair,* 78% mohair/13% wool/9% nylon yarn, medium, worsted weight, 100g = approx. 190yd/174m per hank, color #58 Renaissance

(C) 2 hanks of Colinette Yarns' *Wigwam,* 100% cotton tape yarn, medium, worsted weight, 100g = approx 140yd/128m per hank, color #85 Jay

(D) 2 hanks of Colinette Yarns' *Prism,* 70% wool/30% cotton yarn, bulky, chunky weight, 100g = approx 125yd/114m per hank, color #55 Toscana

(E) 3 hanks of Colinette Yarns' *Zanziba,* 50% wool/50% viscose yarn, medium, worsted weight, 100g = approx 98yd/90m per hank, color #127 Morocco

a painter's palette

Take a closer look. You might guess that the afghan was made with multiple colors, but only two variegated yarns were used to create this diamond lace pattern. This light and airy afghan is a perfect project for showing off your artistic talents.

SKILL LEVEL
Intermediate

Finished Measurements

36 x 59"/91 x 150 cm, blocked

Yarn

Approx total: 1488 yd/1361m
   cotton/rayon blend, lightweight yarn

Color A: 465 yd/425m in gray

Color B: 1023 yd/935m in pink

Materials

Knitting needles: 5.5mm (size 9 U.S.)
   or size to obtain gauge

Tapestry needle for weaving the ends

Gauge

20 sts and 22 rows = 4"/10cm over St st
Always take time to check your gauge.

Pattern Note

The pink section has eight vertical
lace diamonds. The gray section has
1½ vertical lace diamonds on each end.

Special Abbreviations

2-st right twist [RT]: K2tog, leaving
   both sts on needle; insert RH needle
   between 2 sts, and k first st again;
   then sl both sts from needle.

2-st left twist [LT]: With RH needle
   behind LH needle, skip the first st
   and k second st tbl, insert RH needle
   into backs of both sts, k2tog tbl.

Skp: Slip one stitch. Knit next stitch and
   pass slip stitch over knit stitch.

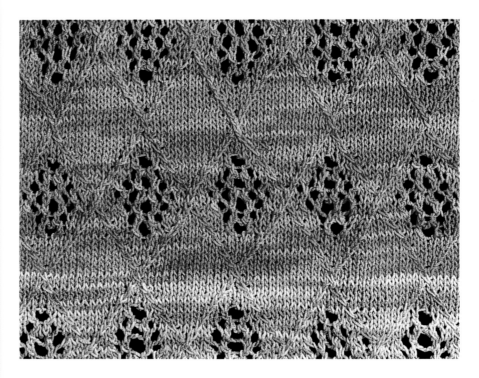

Pattern Stitch

PAINTER'S PALETTE LACE STITCH (CHART A)

Row 1(WS) and every other row: Purl
each st, [k1, p1] in double yo from
previous row.

Row 2 (RS): K4, *[yo, skp] twice, [k2tog,
yo] twice, k2, RT, k2; rep from *, end
last repeat k4 instead of k2, RT, k2.

Row 4: K1, *LT, k1, [k2tog, yo] twice,
[yo, skp] twice, k1, RT; rep from *,
end k1.

Row 6: K1, *k1, LT, k2, yo, skp, k2tog,
yo, k2, RT, k1; rep from *, end k1.

Row 8: K1, *k2, LT, k1, k2tog, [yo] twice,
skp, k1, RT, k2; rep from *, end k1.

Row 10: K1, *k3, LT, k4, RT, k3; rep
from *, end k1.

Design Tip

This afghan is perfect for a knitter
who wants to experiment with
lace and color changing.

Row 12: K1, *k4, LT, k2, RT, k4; rep
from *, end k1.

Row 14: K1, *k5, LT, RT, k5; rep
from *, end k1.

Row 16: K1, *k6, LT, k6; rep from *,
end k1.

Row 18: K1, *k5, RT, LT, k5; rep
from *, end k1.

Row 20: K1, *k4, RT, k2, LT, k4; rep
from *, end k1.

Row 22: K1, *k3, RT, k4, LT, k3; rep
from *, end k1.

Chart A

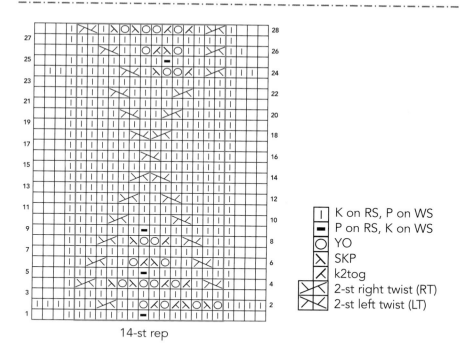

14-st rep

$\vert$	K on RS, P on WS
$-$	P on RS, K on WS
O	YO
$\diagdown$	SKP
$\diagup$	k2tog
	2-st right twist (RT)
	2-st left twist (LT)

Row 24: K3, *RT, k1, k2tog, [yo] twice, skp, k1, LT, k4; rep from *, end last repeat with k3 instead of k4.

Row 26: K2, *RT, k2, yo, skp, k2tog, yo, k2, LT, k2; rep from *.

Row 28: K1, *RT, k1, [k2tog, yo] twice, [yo, skp] twice, k1, LT; rep from *, end k1.

Rep rows 1–28 for pat.

SEED STITCH

Row 1(RS): *K1, p1; rep from * across.

Row 2: P the knit sts and k the purl sts.

Rep row 2 for seed st.

Afghan

With A, CO 164 stitches. With A, work four rows in the seed stitch. Work rows 2–28 once and rows 1–17 once more from the pattern, keeping four border stitches at the beginning and end of each row in the seed stitch throughout. Change to B, and continue from row 18 until completing eight pink lace diamonds vertically, ending with row 17. Change to A, complete rows 18–28 and rows 1–28 once more. Work four rows in the seed stitch. Bind off all stitches.

Finishing

Weave ends in. Block lightly.

This afghan was knit with:

(A) 5 hanks of Classic Elite Yarns' *Imagine*, 53% cotton/47% rayon yarn, light, DK weight, 50g = approx 93 yards per hank, color #9204

(B) 11 hanks of Classic Elite Yarns' *Imagine*, 53% cotton/47% rayon yarn , light, DK weight, 50g = approx 93 yards per hank, color # 9202

counterpane classic

Counterpanes were traditionally knitted in white cotton yarn and made into bed coverings.
In order to retain a classical look, we designed an afghan that preserves the charm of a traditional coverlet with a contemporary twist.

Finished Measurements

43 x 56"/109 x 142cm with crochet border, blocked

Yarn

Approx total: 1824yd/1668m cotton/viscose/silk blend, lightweight yarn

Materials

Knitting needles: 4mm (Size 6 U.S.) *or size to obtain gauge*

Tapestry needle for sewing the seams

Size D-3/3.25mm crochet hook for making the edging

Gauge

21 sts and 26 rows = 4"/10cm over St st
Always take time to check your gauge.

Pattern Note

There are eight rows with six counterpane squares each for a total of 48 squares in the afghan.

Special Abbreviations

Make one stitch (M1): Increase by knitting the top of the st of the previous row.

Inc 5: Knit in front and back of next stitch five times

Rnd: Round

Skp: Slip one stitch. Knit next stitch and pass the slip stitch over the knit stitch.

Sk2p: On RS, Slip one stitch, knit two stitches together. Pass the slipped stitch over two stitches knit together. On WS, slip the next two sts knitwise. Slip these two sts back to LH without twisting them and purl them together through the back loops.

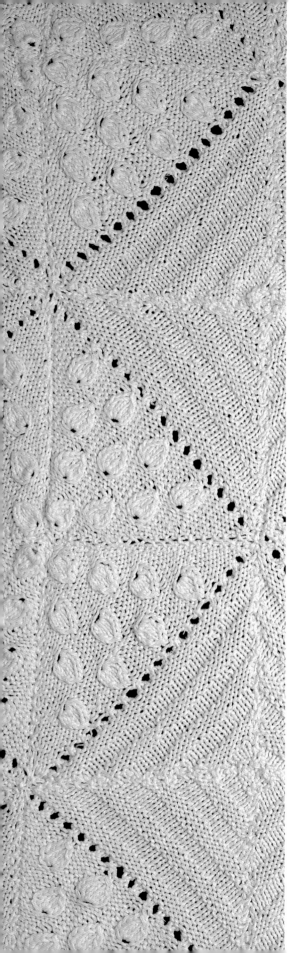

Pattern Stitch

COUNTERPANE SQUARE (CHART A)

Row 1 (WS): K3.

Row 2 (RS): P3.

Row 3: M1, k3, M1. (5 sts)

Row 4: P2, Inc 5, p2. (9 sts)

Row 5: M1, k2, p5, k2, M1. (11 sts)

Row 6: P3, k5, p3.

Row 7: M1, k3, p5, k3, M1. (13 sts)

Row 8: P4, skp, k1, k2tog, p4.

Row 9: M1, k4, p3, k4, M1. (13 sts)

Row 10: P5, sk2p, p5.

Row 11: M1, k11, M1. (13 sts)

Row 12: P3, inc 5, p5, inc 5, p3. (21 sts)

Row 13: M1, k3, p5, k5, p5, k3, M1. (23 sts)

Row 14: P4, k5, p5, k5, p4.

Row 15: M1, k4, p5, k5, p5, k4, M1. (25 sts)

Row 16: [P5, skp, k1, k2tog] twice, p5.

Row 17: M1, [k5, p3] twice, k5, M1. (23 sts)

Row 18: P6, sk2p, p5, sk2p, p6.

Row 19: M1, k19, M1. (21 sts)

Row 20: P4, [inc 5, p5] twice, inc 5, p4. (33 sts)

Row 21: M1, k4, [p5, k5] twice, p5, k4, M1. (35 sts)

Row 22: [P5, k5] 3 times, p5.

Row 23: M1, [k5, p5] 3 times, k5, M1. (37 sts)

Row 24: P6, [skp, k1, k2tog, p5] twice, [skp, k1, k2tog], p6. (31 sts)

Row 25: M1, k6, [p3, k5] twice, p3, k6, M1. (33 sts)

Row 26: P7, [sk2p, p5] twice, sk2p, p7. (27 sts)

Row 27: M1, k27, M1. (29 sts)

Row 28: [P5, inc 5] 4 times, p5. (45 sts)

Row 29: M1, [k5, p5] 4 times, k5, M1. (47 sts)

Row 30: P6, [k5, p5] 3 times, k5, p6.

Row 31: M1, k6, [p5, k5] 3 times, p5, k6, M1. (49 sts)

Row 32: P7, [skp, k1, k2tog, p5] 3 times, [skp, k1, k2tog], p7. (41 sts)

Row 33: M1, k7, [p3, k5] 3 times, p3, k7, M1. (43 sts)

Row 34: P8, [sk2p, p5] 3 times, sk2p, p8. (35 sts)

Row 35: M1, k35, M1. (37 sts)

Row 36: K1, [yo, k2tog] 18 times.

Row 37: Purl.

Row 38: Purl.

Row 39: Skp, k33, k2tog. (35 sts)

Row 40: Purl.

Row 41: Skp, k31, k2tog. (33 sts)

Row 42: Knit.

Row 43: Skp, p29, p2tog. (31 sts)

Row 44: Knit.

Row 45: Skp, p27, p2tog. (29 sts)

Row 46: Purl.

Row 47: Skp, k25, k2tog. (27 sts)

Row 48: Purl.

Row 49: Skp, k23, k2tog. (25 sts)

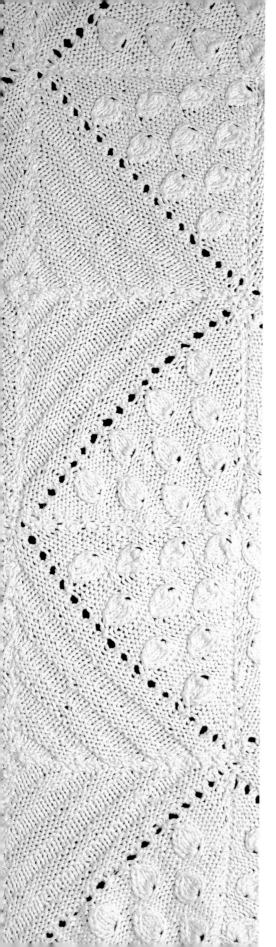

Chart A

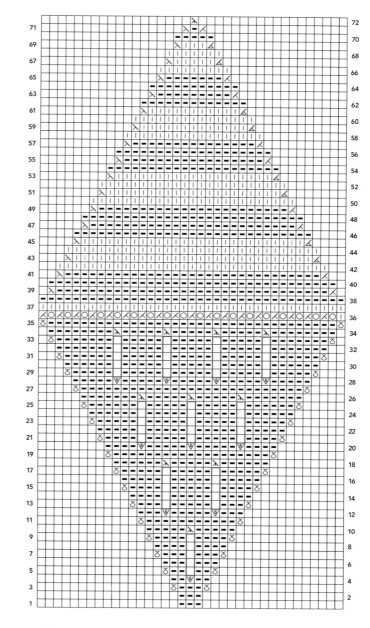

	K on RS, P on WS
—	P on RS, K on WS
○	YO
⊗	M1
⋌	K2tog
⋋	P2tog
⋋	SKP
⋏	Sk2p
⑤	Inc 5

Insert for square chart

	⎮	⎮	⎮	
	⋋	⎮	⋌	
⎮	⎮	⎮	⎮	⎮
⎮	⎮	⎮	⎮	⎮

Rows 5–9
Rows 13–17
Rows 21–25
Rows 29–33

Row 50: Knit.

Row 51: Skp, p21, p2tog. (23 sts)

Row 52: Knit.

Row 53: Skp, p19, p2tog. (21 sts)

Row 54: Purl.

Row 55: Skp, k17, k2tog. (19 sts)

Row 56: Purl.

Row 57: Skp, k15, k2tog. (17 sts)

Row 58: Knit.

Row 59: Skp, p13, p2tog. (15 sts)

Row 60: Knit.

Row 61: Skp, p11, p2tog. (13 sts)

Row 62: Purl.

Row 63: Skp, k9, k2tog. (11 sts)

Row 64: Purl.

Row 65: Skp, k7, k2tog. (9 sts)

Row 66: Knit.

Row 67: Skp, p5, p2tog. (7 sts)

Row 68: Knit.

Row 69: Skp, p3, p2tog. (5 sts)

Row 70: Purl.

Row 71: Skp, k1, k2tog.

Row 72: Sk2p

Work rows 1–72 once for counterpane square.

Counterpane Squares

Make 48. CO 3 stitches. Work the counterpane pattern. Bind off all stitches.

Joining Squares

Block squares to 6½ x 6½"/16.5 x 16.5cm. Seam the squares together using mattress stitch according to the placement diagram.

Finishing

Weave the ends in. Block lightly.

Edging

The general instructions for crocheting are on page 21.

Rnd 1: With RS facing, crochet hook and yarn, work 1 rnd dc evenly around outside edge of afghan.

Rnd 2: Sl st in first st, ch 3, skip 1 st, dc in next dc, *(ch 1, skip 1 dc, dc in next dc), rep from * around.

Rnd 3: Sl st in first st, ch 3, *(dc in ch 1 space, dc in next dc), rep from * around.

Rnd 4: Chain 3, *skip 5 sts, 1 dc in next st, [ch 1, 1 dc in the same st] twice, chain 3 and repeat from * evenly around.

Rnd 5: *1 sc in ch, ch 2, 1 dc in first ch of shell, ch 4, dc in next ch, ch 4, dc in next ch, ch 3, repeat from * evenly around.

Design Tip

To make seaming the squares easier, place them side by side according to the placement diagram when blocking. This will help the edges of the squares conform to each other.

Placement Diagram

Counterpane square

This afghan was knit with:

(A) 16 skeins of Dale of Norway Yarn's *Svale,* 50% cotton/40% viscose/ 10% silk, light, DK weight 1.75 oz/50 g= approx 114 yd/104 m per skein, color #0020

autumn twilight

This afghan is knit with two strands of mohair yarn worked together in a simple cell stitch. The result is a light throw that is also wonderfully warm. The yarn, with its shades of autumn and a flash of vivid blue, make it perfect for fall evenings by the fireplace.

Finished Measurements

40 x 50"/102 x 127cm

Yarn

Approx total: 1312yd/1200m mohair/viscose/polyester blend, medium weight yarn

Color A: 984yd/900m in brown

Color B: 328yd/300m in blue

Materials

Knitting needles: 9mm (Size 13 U.S.) *or size to obtain gauge*

Tapestry needle for weaving the ends.

Large crochet hook for attaching the fringe

Cardboard strip, 5"/12.7cm wide, for making the fringe

Gauge

12 sts = 4"/10cm over St st using 2 strands of A or B

Always take time to check your gauge.

Pattern Note

For Color AA, hold two strands of A.

For Color BB, hold two strands of B.

After every 18 rows, two rows will be worked in BB.

Special Abbreviations

Skp: Slip one stitch. Knit next stitch and pass the slip stitch over the knit stitch.

Sk2p: Slip one stitch, knit two stitches together. Pass the slipped stitch over two stitches knit together.

Pattern Stitch

AUTUMN TWILIGHT STITCH (CHART A)

Row 1 (RS): K2, *yo, sk2p, yo, k1; rep from * to last st, k1.

Rows 2 and 4: Purl.

Row 3: K1, k2tog, yo, k1, *yo, sk2p, yo, k1; rep from * to last 3 sts, yo, skp, k1.

Rep rows 1–4 for pat.

Design Tip

You can knit with three strands to make a heavier afghan.

Afghan

With AA, CO 83 stitches. Work two rows in the garter stitch. Work rows 1–4 four times. *Change to BB, work rows 1 and 2 once. Change to AA, work rows 3 and 4 once and rows 1–4 four times. Repeat from * until the afghan measures 49½"/126 cm. With AA, work two rows in the garter stitch. Bind off all stitches.

Finishing

Weave in the ends.

Fringe

The general instructions for making fringe are on page 20. Using Color B, wrap it six times around the width of the cardboard strip for each of the fringes. Make enough fringes to attach to both of the short edges of the afghan.

Chart A

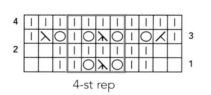

4-st rep

	K on RS, P on WS
O	YO
⟋	K2tog
⟍	SKP
⋏	Sk2p

This afghan was knit with:

(A) 6 balls of Artful Yarns' *Portrait*, 70% mohair/25% viscose/5% polyester yarn, medium, worsted weight, 50g = approx 164yd/150m per ball, color #104

(B) 2 balls of Artful Yarns' *Portrait*, 70% mohair/25% viscose/5% polyester yarn, medium, worsted weight, 50g = approx 164yd/150m per ball, color #103

era

This timeless, elegant afghan displays a design of cabled lace and delicate bobbles that can be knit in any color. If you're eager to show off your skills, this is the perfect project.

SKILL LEVEL
Experienced

Finished Measurements

45 x 65"/114 x 165cm

Yarn

Approx total: 1710yd/1564m wool/mohair blend, medium weight yarn

Materials

Knitting needles: 6.0mm (Size 10 U.S.) *or size to obtain gauge*

Cable needles

Tapestry needle for weaving the ends

Large crochet hook for attaching the fringe

Cardboard strip, 9"/23cm wide, for making the fringe

Gauge

16 sts = 4"/10 cm over St st
Always take time to check your gauge.

Special Abbreviations

Skp: Slip one stitch. Knit next stitch and pass the slip stitch over knit stitch.

Make Bobble (MB): [K1, p1, k1, p1, k1, p1, k1] in the next stitch, making 7 stitches from one; then pass the 6th, 5th, 4th, 3rd, 2nd , and first stitch over the last stitch made.

9-st right cable: Sl 4 stitches to the cable needle and hold to the back of the work, k5, k4 from the cable needle.

Design Tip

You can add beads in place of the bobbles for an elegant look.

Pattern Stitch

ERA STITCH (CHART A)

Row 1 (RS): *K4, yo, skp, p7, k2tog, yo, k3, rep from * to last 19 sts, k4, yo, skp, p7, k2tog, yo, p4.

Rows 2, 4, and 6: P the yo and purl sts, k the knit sts.

Row 3: *K3, [yo, skp] twice, p5, [k2tog, yo] twice, k2, rep from * to last 19 sts, k3, [yo, skp] twice, p5, [k2tog, yo] twice, k3.

Row 5: *K2, [yo, skp] 3 times, p3, [k2tog, yo] 3 times, k1, rep from * to last 19 sts, k2, [yo, skp] 3 times, p3, [k2tog, yo] 3 times, k2.

Row 7: *K1, [yo, skp] 4 times, k1, [k2tog, yo] 4 times, rep from * to last 19 sts, k1, [yo, skp] 4 times, k1, [k2tog, yo] 4 times, k1.

Row 8: *[K2, p15, k1], rep from * to last 19 sts, k2, p15, k2.

Row 9: *P2, [yo, skp] 3 times, k3, [k2tog, yo] 3 times, p1, rep from * to last 19 sts, p2 [yo, skp] 3 times, k3, [k2tog, yo] 3 times, p2.

Row 10: *[K3, p13, k2] rep from * to last 19 sts, k3, p13, k3.

Row 11: *P3, [yo, skp] twice, k5, [k2tog, yo] twice, p2, rep from * to last 19 sts, p3, [yo, skp] twice, k5, [k2tog, yo] twice, p3.

Row 12: *[K4, p11, k3], rep from * to last 19 sts, k4, p11, k4.

Row 13: *P4, yo, skp, k7, k2tog, yo, p3, rep from * to last 19 sts, p4, yo, skp, k7, k2tog, yo, p4.

Rows 14, 16, and 18: *[K5, p9, k4], rep from * to last 19 sts, k5, p9, k5.

Chart A

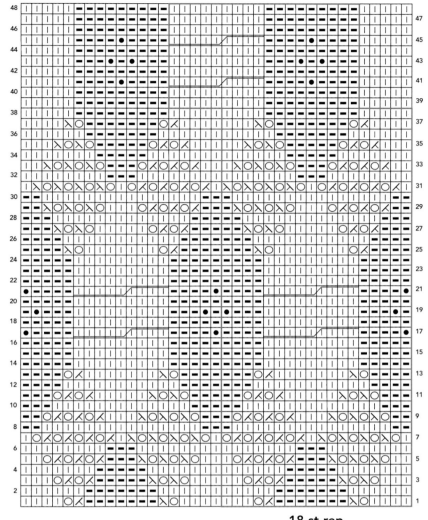

18-st rep

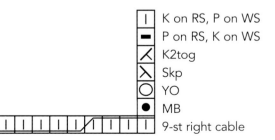

	K on RS, P on WS
—	P on RS, K on WS
⋋	K2tog
⋌	Skp
○	YO
●	MB

9-st right cable

Row 15: *[P5, k9, p4] rep from * to last 19 sts, p5, k9, p5.

Rows 17: *MB, p4, 9-st right cable, p4, rep from * to last 19 sts, MB, p4, 9-st right cable, p4, MB.

Row 19: *P1, MB, p3, k9, p3, MB, rep from * to last 19 sts, p1, MB, p3, k9, p3, MB, p1.

Rows 20, 22, and 24: Rep row 14.

Row 21: Rep row 17.

Row 23: Rep row 15.

Row 25: *P4, k2tog, yo, k7, yo, skp, p3, rep from * to last 19 sts, p4, k2tog, yo, k7, yo, skp, p4.

Rows 26, 28, and 30: Rep row 2.

Row 27: *P3, [k2tog, yo] twice, k5, [yo, skp] twice, p2, rep from * to last 19 sts, p3, [k2tog, yo] twice, k5, [yo, skp] twice, p3.

Row 29: *P2, [k2tog, yo] 3 times, k3, [yo, skp] 3 times, p1, rep from * to last 19 sts, p2, [k2tog, yo] 3 times, k3, [yo, skp] 3 times, p2.

Row 31: *K1, [k2tog, yo] 4 times, k1, [yo, skp] 4 times, rep from * to last 19 sts, k1, [k2tog, yo] 4 times, k1, [yo, skp] 4 times, k1.

Row 32: *P8, k3, p7, rep from * to last 19 sts, p8, k3, p8.

Row 33: *K2, [k2tog, yo] 3 times, p3, [yo, skp] 3 times, k1, rep from * to last 19 sts, k2, [k2tog, yo] 3 times, p3, [yo, skp] 3 times, k2.

Row 34: *P7, k5, p6, rep from * to last 19 sts, p7, k5, p7.

Row 35: *K3, [k2tog, yo] twice, p5, [yo, skp] twice, k2, rep from * to last 19 sts, k3, [k2tog, yo] twice, p5, [yo, skp] twice, k3.

Row 36: *P6, k7, p5 rep from * to last 19 sts, p6, k7, p6.

Row 37: *K4, k2tog, yo, p7, yo, skp, k3, rep from * to last 19 sts, k4, k2tog, yo, p7, yo, skp, k4.

Rows 38, 40, and 42: P5, *k9, p9, rep from * to last 14 sts, k9, p5.

Row 39: K5, *p9, k9, rep from * to last 14 sts, p9, k5.

Row 41: K5, *p4, MB, p4, 9-st right cable, rep from * to last 14 sts, p4, MB, p4, k5.

Row 43: K5, *p3, MB, p1, MB, p3, k9, rep from * to last 14 sts, p3, MB, p1, MB, p3, k5.

Rows 44, 46, and 48: Rep row 38.

Row 45: Rep row 41.

Row 47: Rep row 39.

Rep rows 1–48 for pat.

SEED STITCH

Row 1 (RS): *K1, p1; rep from * across.

Row 2: P the knit sts and k the purl sts.

Rep row 2 for seed st.

Afghan

CO 189 stitches. Work three rows in the seed stitch. Work in the pattern, keeping four stitches at the beginning and end of the row in the seed stitch. Work as established until the afghan measures approximately 64½"/164 cm from the beginning. Work three rows in the seed st. Bind off all sts.

Finishing

Weave the ends in. Block.

Knotted Fringe

The general instructions for making knotted fringe are on page 20. For each of the fringes, wrap the yarn eight times around the width of the cardboard strip. Make enough fringes to place them 1"/2.5cm apart across the edges of afghan. Work the second level of knots close to the first level. Work the third level close to the second level. Trim the ends. Repeat for the other edge.

This afghan was knit with:

9 skeins of Brown Sheep Company's *Lamb's Pride*, 85% wool/15% mohair yarn, medium, worsted weight, 4oz/ 112g = approx 190yd/173m per skein, color #M-18 Khaki

silky lights

This wonderfully lightweight afghan is intricately knit with three shades of gorgeous silk-cotton blend yarn. Made in lace and bobbles, the soft bands of color are reminiscent of candlelight reflected on walls of polished wood.

SKILL LEVEL
Experienced

Finished Measurements

55 x 55"/140 x 140cm, blocked

Yarn

Approx total: 1888yd/1726m
silk/cotton blend, medium
weight yarn

Color A: 708yd/647m in white

Color B: 590yd/540m in light brown

Color C: 590yd/540m in dark brown

Materials

Knitting needles: 5.5mm
(Size 9 U.S.) *or size to obtain gauge*

Tapestry needle for weaving the ends

Large crochet hook for attaching
the fringe

Cardboard strip, 9"/23cm wide,
for making the fringe

Gauge

18 sts = 4"/10cm over St st
Always take time to check your gauge.

Pattern Note

There are five horizontal color panels
of B and C, and six horizontal color
panels of A.

Each color section is worked
over 18 rows.

Special Abbreviations

Make Bobble (MB): [K1, p1, k1, p1, k1,
p1, k1] in the next st, making 7 sts
from one; then pass the 6th, 5th, 4th,
3rd, 2nd and first st over the
last st made.

Skp: Slip one stitch. Knit next stitch
and pass the slipped stitch over the
knit stitch.

Sk2p: Slip one stitch, knit two stitches
together. Pass the slipped stitch over
two stitches knit together.

Pattern Stitch

SILKY LIGHTS STITCH (CHART A)

Row 1 (RS): P6, *k2, skp, yo, MB, yo,
k2tog, k2, p11, rep from *, end last
repeat p6 instead of p11.

Row 2 (WS) and all even rows: K the
yo and knit sts, p the purl sts.

Row 3: P6, *k1, k2tog, yo, k3, yo, skp,
k1, p11, rep from *, end last repeat p6
instead of p11.

Row 5: P2tog, *p4, k2, yo, k2tog, yo,
MB, yo, skp, yo, k2, p4, p3tog, rep
from *, end last repeat p2tog instead of
p3tog.

Row 7: P2tog, *p3, k2, yo, k2tog, [k1,
yo] twice, k1, skp, yo, k2, p3, p3tog,
rep from *, end last repeat p2tog
instead of p3tog.

Row 9: P2tog, *p2, k2, yo, k2tog, k2,
yo, MB, yo, k2, skp, yo, k2, p2, p3tog,
rep from *, end last repeat p2tog
instead of p3tog.

Row 11: P2tog, *p1, k2, yo, k2tog, k2,
p1, yo, k1, yo, p1, k2, skp, yo, k2, p1,
p3tog, rep from *, end last repeat
p2tog instead of p3tog.

Row 13: P2tog, *k2, yo, k2tog, k2, p2,
yo, MB, yo, p2, k2, skp, yo, k2, p3tog,
rep from *, end last repeat p2tog
instead of p3tog.

Row 15: K2tog, *k1, yo, k2tog, k2, p3,
yo, k1, yo, p3, k2, skp, yo, k1, sk2p,
rep from *, end last repeat skp instead
of sk2p.

Row 17: Skp, *yo, k2tog, k2, p4, yo,
MB, yo, p4, k2, skp, yo, sk2p, rep
from *, end last repeat k2tog instead
of sk2p.

Row 19: K1, *yo, k2tog, k2, p11, k2,
skp, yo, MB, rep from *, end last
repeat k1 instead of MB.

Row 21: K2, *yo, skp, k1, p11, k1,
k2tog, yo, k3, rep from *, end last
repeat k2 instead of k3.

Row 23: K1, *yo, skp, yo, k2, p4, p3tog,
p4, k2, yo, k2tog, yo, MB, rep from *,
end last repeat k1 instead of MB.

Row 25: K1, *yo, k1, skp, yo, k2, p3,
p3tog, p3, k2, yo, k2tog, k1, yo, k1,
rep from * to end.

Row 27: K1, *yo, k2, skp, yo, k2, p2,
p3tog, p2, k2, yo, k2tog, k2, yo, MB,
rep from *, end last repeat k1 instead
of MB.

Row 29: K1, *yo, p1, k2, skp, yo, k2,
p1, p3tog, p1, k2, yo, k2tog, k2, p1,
yo, k1, rep from * to end.

Design Tip

To help you remember when the
color changes, mark the graph at
rows 13 and 31.

Chart A

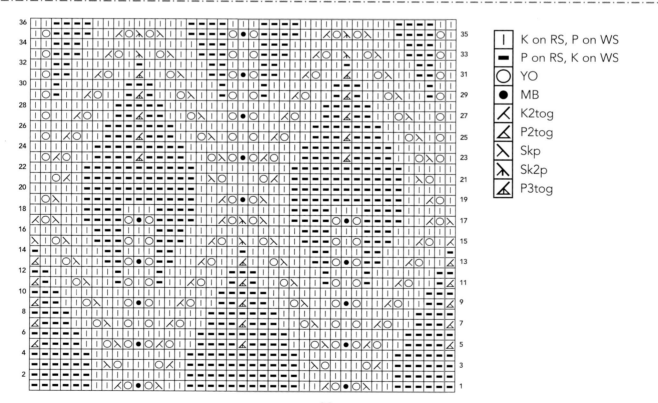

20-st rep

Legend:

Symbol	Description
I	K on RS, P on WS
−	P on RS, K on WS
○	YO
●	MB
⋌	K2tog
⋌	P2tog
⋋	Skp
⋏	Sk2p
⋌	P3tog

Row 31: K1, *yo, p2, k2, skp, yo, k2, p3tog, k2, yo, k2tog, k2, p2, yo, MB, rep from *, end last repeat k1 instead of MB.

Row 33: K1, *yo, p3, k2, skp, yo, k1, sk2p, k1, yo, k2tog, k2, p3, yo, k1, rep from * to end.

Row 35: K1, *yo, p4, k2, skp, yo, sk2p, yo, k2tog, k2, p4, yo, MB, rep from *, end last repeat k1 instead of MB.

Row 36: Work Row 2

Rep Rows 1–36 for pat.

SEED STITCH

Row 1(RS): *K1, p1; rep from * across.

Row 2: P the knit sts and k the purl sts.

Rep row 2 for seed st.

Afghan

With A, CO 209 stitches. Work two rows in the seed stitch. Work rows 1–12 of the pattern in A, keeping four border stitches at the beginning and end of each row in the seed stitch throughout. *Work B for 18 rows, work C for 18 rows, work A for 18 rows, repeat from* four more times. Work two rows in the seed stitch. Bind off all stitches.

Finishing

Weave the ends in. Block.

Knotted Fringe

The general instructions for making knotted fringe are on page 20. Using Colors A, B, and C together, wrap the yarns two times around the width of the cardboard strip. Place fringes 1½"/3.8cm apart along edge of the afghan. Work the second level close to the first level. Repeat for other edge. Each end of the afghan has a two-level knotted fringe.

This afghan was knit with:

(A) 6 hanks of Rowan Yarns' *Summer Tweed*, 70% silk/30% cotton yarn, medium, worsted weight, 50g = approx 118yd/ 108m per hank, color #508

(B) 5 hanks of Rowan Yarns' *Summer Tweed*, 70% silk/30% cotton yarn, medium, worsted weight, 50g = approx 118yd/ 108m per hank, color #515

(C) 5 hanks of Rowan Yarns' *Summer Tweed*, 70% silk/30% cotton yarn, medium, worsted weight, 50g = approx 118yd/ 108m per hank, color #514

sweet honey

Go wild! Add a splash of exuberant texture and color to your knitting with this fun-fur novelty yarn around an easy-to-knit honeycomb center. The lush pompoms accent this afghan for a wild and furry look.

Finished Measurements

31 x 55"/79 x 140cm

Yarn

Color A: Approx total: 595yd/544m polyester, bulky weight yarn

Color B: Approx total: 380yd/347m wool blend, medium weight yarn

Materials

Knitting needles: 6mm (Size 10 U.S.) *or size to obtain gauge*

Cable needle

Tapestry needle for weaving the ends

Large crochet hook for attaching the pompoms

Two cardboard circles, 4"/10cm diameter, for making the pompoms

Gauge

12 sts = 4"/10 cm over St st using strand of Color A

16 sts = 4"/10 cm over St st using strand of Color B

Always take time to check your gauge.

Pattern Note

Work the pattern stitch in Color B.

Special Abbreviations

4-st right cable: Slip 2 stitches to the cable needle and hold to the back of the work, k2, k2 from cn.

4-st left cable: Slip 2 stitches to the cable needle and hold to the front of the work, k2, k2 from cn.

Pattern Stitch

HONEYCOMB STITCH (CHART A)

Row 1 (RS): With B, *4-st right cable, 4-st left cable; rep from* to the end.

Row 2: Purl.

Row 3: Knit.

Row 4: Purl.

Row 5: *4-st left cable, 4-st right cable; rep from* to the end.

Row 6: Purl.

Row 7: Knit.

Row 8: Purl.

Rep rows 1–8 for pat.

Chart A

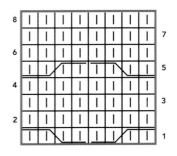

	K on RS, P on WS
	4-st left cable
	4-st right cable

Afghan

With A, CO 112 stitches. Work stock-inette stitch until the afghan measures 14"/35.6cm. Keeping 24 stitches at the beginning and the end of the row in the stockinette stitch in A, begin working from the pattern with B until the pattern measures approx. 26"/66 cm. Change to A, work stockinette stitch 14"/35.6 cm. Bind off all stitches.

Finishing

Weave the ends in.

Pompoms

Make 24 in color B. The general instructions for making pompoms are on page 20. Holding the two circles together, wrap yarn in color B around the cardboard. Repeat for the remaining 23 pompoms. Attach 12 pompoms evenly across each edge. Weave the ends in.

Design Tip

Our mother used to show us how to make pompoms when we were little. Having children help you make the pompoms can make the activity more enjoyable.

This afghan was knit with:

(A) 7 balls of Crystal Palace Yarns' *Splash*, 100% polyester yarn, super bulky, bulky weight, 100g = approx 85yd/78m per ball, color # 7177

(B) 2 skeins of Brown Sheep Company's *Lamb's Pride*, 85% wool/15% mohair yarn, light, worsted weight, 4oz/112g = approx 190yd/174m per skein, color #M-110 Orange You Glad

fascinating rhythm

The mitered diamond design, combined with purl accent rows, gives a visual rhythm to this vividly colored afghan. While the pattern is recommended for intermediate knitters, experienced beginners who dare to challenge their skills will find this a rewarding accomplishment.

Finished Measurements

49 x 60"/125 x 152cm, blocked

Yarn

Approx total: 2958yd/2704m cotton/acrylic blend, medium weight yarn

  Color A: 1479yd/1352m in blue

  Color B: 1479yd/1352m in red

Approx total: 1400yd/1280m rayon/wool blend, medium weight yarn

  Color C: 700yd/640m in red

  Color D: 700yd/640m in gold

Materials

Knitting needles: 5.0mm (Size 8 U.S.) *or size to obtain gauge*

Stitch markers

Tapestry needle for sewing the seams

Large crochet hook for attaching the tassels

Cardboard strip, 6"/15cm wide, for making the tassels

Gauge

16 sts and 24 rows = 4"/10cm over St st using Color A or B

20 sts and 28 rows = 4"/10cm over St st using Color C or D

Always take time to check your gauge.

Design Tip

To bring out your artistic side, and to make this afghan even more colorful, use different colors of leftover yarn.

Pattern Notes

This afghan is made of 32 diamonds and eight half-diamonds.

Special Abbreviations

Skp: Slip one stitch. Knit the next stitch and pass the slip stitch over the knit stitch.

Pattern Stitch

DIAMOND (B)

(Make 20)

With C, CO 60 sts.

Rows 1 & 3 (WS): With C, knit.

Row 2 (RS): With C, k28, k2tog, pm, skp, k to end.

Rows 4 & 6: With A, k to 2 sts before marker, k2tog, sl marker, skp, k to end.

Rows 5 & 7: With A, purl.

Row 8: With C, rep row 4.

Row 9: With C, knit.

Rep rows 4–9 eight times more, then rep rows 4 and 5 until one st remains. Fasten off.

DIAMOND (R)

(Make 12)

With D, CO 60 sts.

Rows 1 & 3 (WS): With D, knit.

Row 2 (RS): With D, k28, k2tog, pm, skp, k to end.

Rows 4 & 6: With B, k to 2 sts before marker, k2tog, sl marker, skp, k to end.

Row 5 & 7: With B, purl.

Row 8: With D, rep row 4.

Row 9: With D, knit.

Rep rows 4–9 eight times more, then rep rows 4 and 5 until one st remains. Fasten off.

HALF DIAMONDS (HR)

(Make 8)

With D, CO 30 sts.

Rows 1 & 3 (WS): With D, knit.

Row 2 (RS): With D, skp, knit across to last two sts, k2tog.

Placement Diagram

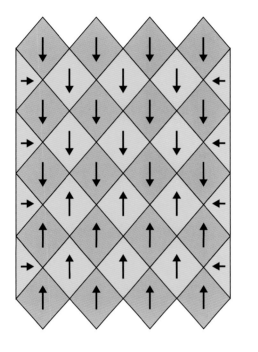

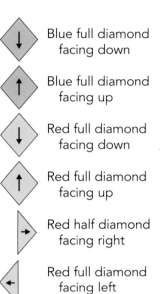

Blue full diamond facing down

Blue full diamond facing up

Red full diamond facing down

Red full diamond facing up

Red half diamond facing right

Red full diamond facing left

Rows 4 & 6: With B, skp, knit across to last two sts, k2tog.

Rows 5 & 7: With B, purl.

Row 8: With D, rep row 4.

Row 9: With D, knit.

Rep rows 4–9 five more times, then rep rows 4 and 5 until one st remains. Fasten off.

Afghan

Seam the diamonds and half-diamonds together according to the placement diagram.

Finishing

Weave the ends in. Block.

Tassels

Make eight. The general instructions for making tassels are on page 20. Using D, wrap the yarn 12 times around the width of the cardboard strip, then wrap the yarn to make the head, leaving a length of yarn for attachment. Using C, wrap around the head of the tassel once more. Trim the edges of each tassel. Attach the tassels across the pointed mitered edges of the afghan.

This afghan was knit with:

(A) 17 hanks of Berroco Yarns' *Optik,* 48% cotton/21% acrylic/ 20% mohair/8% metallic/ 3% polyester yarn, medium, worsted weight, 1.75oz/50g = approx 87yd/80m per hank, color #4905 Tiffany

(B) 17 hanks of Berroco Yarns' *Optik,* 48% cotton/21% acrylic/ 20% mohair/8% metallic/ 3% polyester yarn, medium, worsted weight, 1.75oz/50g = approx 87yd/80m per hank, color #4951 Monsoon

(C) 7 hanks of Berroco Yarns' *Softwist,* 59% rayon/41% wool yarn, medium, worsted weight, 1.75oz/50g = approx 100yd/92m per hank, color #9455 Cool Red

(D) 7 hanks of Berroco Yarns' *Softwist,* 59% rayon/41% wool yarn, medium, worsted weight, 1.75oz/50g = approx 100yd/92m per hank, color #9438 Tupelo Honey

berries in a basket

The traditional basket-weave texture is created with a simple twist-stitch technique that allows you to effortlessly knit without using a cable needle. The gradually deepening bands of color reflect nature's ripening process—a perfect afghan for evening picnics in the park.

Finished Measurements

40 x 60"/102 x152cm, blocked

Yarn

Approx total: 2940yd/2688m wool, medium weight yarn

Color A: 490yd/448m medium pink

Color B: 490yd/448m medium rose

Color C: 490yd/448m deep rose

Color D: 490yd/448m cranberry

Color E: 490yd/448m medium burgundy

Color F: 490yd/448m deep burgundy

Materials

Knitting needles: 5.5mm (Size 9 U.S.) or size to obtain gauge

Tapestry needle for weaving the ends

Large crochet hook for attaching the fringe

Cardboard strip, 5"/12.7cm wide, for making the fringe

Gauge

18 sts and 20 rows = 4"/10cm over St st
Always take time to check your gauge.

Pattern Note

There are six color sections worked in the pattern, each measuring 10"/25cm.

Special Abbreviations

2-st right twist [RT]: K2tog, leaving both sts on needle; insert RH needle between 2 sts, and k first st again; then sl both sts from needle.

2-st left twist [LT]: With RH needle behind LH needle, skip the first st and k second st tbl, insert RH needle into backs of both sts, k2tog tbl.

Pattern Stitch

BERRIES LATTICE STITCH (CHART A)

Row 1 and all WS rows: K2, purl across to last 2 sts, k2.

Row 2: K2, *LT, [RT] twice; rep from *, end LT, RT, k2.

Row 4: K3, LT, *RT, [LT] twice; rep from *, end k3.

Row 6: K2, [LT] twice, *k2; [LT] twice; rep from *, end k2.

Row 8: K3, *[LT] twice, RT; rep from *, end LT, k3.

Row 10: K2, RT, *LT, [RT] twice; rep from *, end LT, k2.

Row 12: K5, *[RT] twice, k2; rep from *, end k3.

Rep Rows 1–12 for pat.

Design Tip

The stitch makes this afghan roll up slightly on the edges. If you prefer a straight edge, add more garter stitches to the border.

Chart A

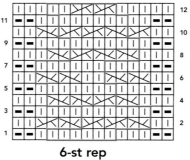

6-st rep

I	K on RS, P on WS
—	P on RS, K on WS
⧄	2-st RT
⧅	2-st LT

Afghan

CO 176 stitches. With A, work in the pattern until the afghan measures 10"/25.4 cm. Change to B and *work as established until completing 10"/25.4cm from the previous color. Repeat from * for C, D, E, and F. Bind off all stitches.

Finishing

Weave the ends in. Block lightly.

Fringe

The general instructions for making fringe are on page 20. Make 20 fringes for each color by wrapping each six times around the width of the cardboard strip. Attach 10 fringes in color A on one edge of the afghan; repeat using the remaining five colors of fringe across edge. Repeat for other edge.

This afghan was knit with:

(A) 2 skeins of Brown Sheep Company's *Nature Spun*, 100% wool, medium worsted weight, 3.5oz/100g = approx 245yd/224m per skein, color #N87 Victorian Pink

(B) 2 skeins of Brown Sheep Company's *Nature Spun*, 100% wool, medium worsted weight, 3.5oz/100g = approx 245yd/224m per skein, color #N98 Pink Please

(C) 2 skeins of Brown Sheep Company's *Nature Spun*, 100% wool, medium, worsted weight, 3.5oz/100g = approx 245yd/224m per skein, color #N99 Pagan Pink

(D) 2 skeins of Brown Sheep Company's *Nature Spun*, 100% wool, medium, worsted weight, 3.5oz/100g= approx. 245yd/224m per skein, color #N81 Cranberry Fog

(E) 2 skeins of Brown Sheep Company's *Nature Spun*, 100% wool, medium, worsted weight, 3.5oz/100g = approx 245yd/224m per skein, color #235 Beet Red

(F) 2 skeins of Brown Sheep Company's *Nature Spun*, 100% wool, medium, worsted weight, 3.5oz/100g = approx 245yd/224m per skein, color #N40 Grape Harvest

bold heritage

This afghan creates a lasting impression—almost as if you're walking back in time through an ancient civilization. The motifs are made using duplicate stitch. With only three colors of yarn and a simple knitted background, this project is perfect for an experienced beginner.

SKILL LEVEL
Easy

Finished Measurements

44 x 50"/112 x 127cm, blocked

Yarn

Approx total: 1936yd/1771m wool, medium weight yarn

Color A: 704yd/644m in black

Color B: 352yd/322m in red

Color C: 880yd/805m in gold

Materials

Knitting needles: 5.0mm (Size 8 U.S.) *or size to obtain gauge*

Tapestry needle for the duplicate stitch and weaving the ends

Large crochet hook for attaching the tassels

Cardboard strip, 5"/12.7cm wide, for making the tassels

Gauge

17 sts = 4"/10cm over St st
Always take time to check your gauge.

Pattern Note

The center of the afghan is knit in Color C, while the outer border is knit in Color A. The border motifs will be duplicate stitched in Colors B and C. The center motif will be duplicate stitched in Colors A and B starting from stitch 48 on row 47.

Pattern Stitch

SEED STITCH

Row 1 (RS): *K1, p1; rep from * across.

Row 2: P the knit sts and k the purl sts.

Rep row 2 for seed st.

Afghan

With A, CO 169 stitches. Work four rows in the seed stitch.

Row 1: *Work seed st over 4 sts, k29, rep from* 4 more times, work seed st over 4 sts.

Row 2: *Work seed st over 4 sts, p29, rep from* 4 more times, work seed st over 4 sts.

Rep rows 1–2 13 more times, and rep row 1 once more.

Work 4 rows in seed stitch.

Row 34: Work seed st over 4 sts, p29, work seed st over 4 sts. Change to C, p95 sts. Change to A, work seed st over 4 sts, p29, work seed st over 4 sts.

Row 35: Work seed st over 4 sts, k29, work seed st over 4 sts. Change to C, k95 sts. Change to A, work seed st over 4 sts, k29, work seed st over 4 sts.

Rep rows 34 and 35 thirteen more times, and rep row 34 once more.

Row 63: Work seed st over 37 sts. Change to C, k95 sts. Change to A, work seed st over 37 sts.

Design Tip

If you make any mistakes on the duplicate stitches, you can use the main background color to camouflage them.

Chart A

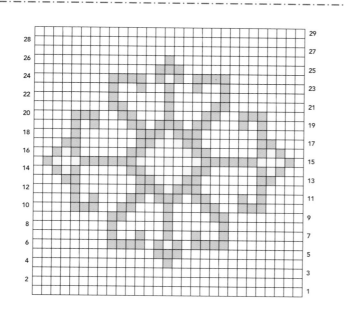

Chart B

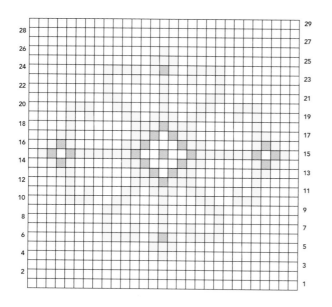

Row 64: Work seed st over 37 sts. Change to C, p95 sts. Change to A, work seed st over 37 sts.

Repeat rows 63 and 64 once more.

Row 67: Work seed st over 4 sts, k29, work seed st over 4 sts. Change to C, k95 sts. Change to A, work seed st over 4 sts, k29, work seed st over 4 sts.

Row 68: Work seed st over 4 sts, p29, work seed st over 4 sts. Change to C, p95 sts. Change to A, work seed st over 4 sts, p29, work seed st over 4 sts.

Rep rows 67 and 68 thirteen more times, and rep row 67 once more.

Row 96: Repeat row 64.

Row 97: Repeat row 63.

Rep rows 96 and 97 once more.

Rep rows 34–99 two more times.

Rep rows 1–2 fourteen more times, and rep row 1 once.

Work 4 rows in seed st.

Bind off.

Chart C

Finishing

Weave the ends in. Block the afghan lightly. Following the general instructions for duplicate stitch on page 17, work the duplicate stitch embroidery on the afghan following the charts and placement diagram.

Tassels

Make two. The general instructions for making tassels are on page 20. Using B, wrap the yarn 15 times around the width of the cardboard strip, then wrap the yarn to make the head, leaving a length of yarn for attachment. Trim the edges of each tassel. Attach the tassels at each end of the Central Motif's small diamond.

This afghan was knit with:

(A) 8 skeins of Dale of Norway Yarn's *Free Style Dalegarn*, 100% wool, medium, worsted weight, 1oz/50g = approx 88yd/80m per skein, color #0090

(B) 4 skeins of Dale of Norway Yarn's *Free Style Dalegarn*, 100% wool, medium, worsted weight, 1oz/50g = approx 88yd/80m per skein, color #4018

(C) 10 skeins of Dale of Norway Yarn's *Free Style Dalegarn*, 100% wool, medium, worsted weight, 1oz/50g = approx 88yd/80m per skein, color #2427

Placement Diagram

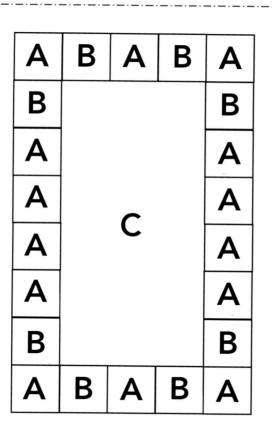

A   Red Side Motif (chart A)

B   Yellow Side Motif (chart B)

C   Center Motif (chart C)

radiant ruby

Ruby red yarn combines with multi-colored fluorescent threads to create a stunning lacy afghan that radiates elegance. Requiring a sophisticated combination of stitches, this project is exhilarating for both experienced knitters and intrepid beginners willing to stretch their skills.

Finished Measurements

35 x 52"/89 x 132cm, blocked

Yarn

Color A: Approx total: 546yd/499m nylon, medium weight yarn

Color B: Approx total: 900yd/823m rayon/wool blend, medium weight yarn

Materials

Knitting needles: 6mm (Size 10 U.S.) *or size to obtain gauge*

Tapestry needle for weaving the ends

Large crochet hook for attaching the fringe

Cardboard strip, 5"/12.7cm wide, for making the fringe

Gauge

16 sts and 20 rows = 4"/10cm over St st using Color A and B tog
Always take time to check your gauge.

Pattern Note

For Color AB, hold one strand of A and B together. For Color B, hold one strand of B.

Special Abbreviations

Skp: Slip one stitch. Knit next stitch and pass the slip stitch over the knit stitch.

Sk2p: Slip one stitch, knit two stitches together. Pass the slipped stitch over two stitches knit together.

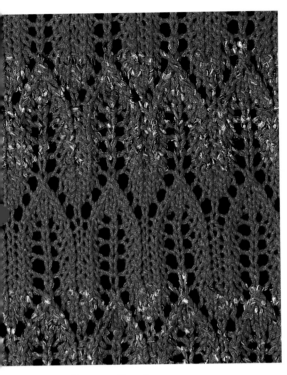

Pattern Stitch

RADIANT RUBY LACE STITCH

Row 1 and all WS: K4, purl across to last 4 sts, k4.

Row 2: K5, *yo, skp, k3, k2tog, yo, k1, rep from* to end, k4.

Row 4: K6, *yo, skp, k1, k2tog, yo, k3, rep from*, end last repeat k6.

Row 6: K4, p1, *k2, yo, sk2p, yo, k2, p1, rep from* to end, k4.

Rows 8, 10, 12, 14, and 16: K4, p1, *skp, (k1, yo) twice, k1, k2tog, p1, rep from* to end, k4.

Rep rows 1–16 for lace pat.

Design Tip

Bamboo needles work great with nylon yarn.

Afghan

With AB, CO 110 sts. Work four rows in the garter stitch. Work row 1 of pat. *With AB, work rows 2–16 once and row 1 once more from the lace pattern. Change to B, work rows 2–16 once and row 1 once more; repeat from* until the afghan measures 51½"/131cm. Work four rows in thegarter stitch. Bind off all stitches.

Finishing

Weave the ends in. Block.

Knotted Fringe

The general instructions for making knotted fringe are on page 20. Make enough fringes to alternate the colors below the pointed edge of the leaf pattern so they are 3½"/8.9cm apart. For each color, wrap the yarn seven times around the width of the cardboard strip. Attach the fringe and knot the second level close to the first level. Trim the ends.

Chart A

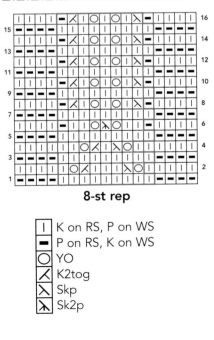

8-st rep

I	K on RS, P on WS	
-	P on RS, K on WS	
O	YO	
⟋	K2tog	
⟍	Skp	
⅄	Sk2p	

This afghan was knit with:

(A) 7 balls of Berroco Yarns' *Mosaic FX*, 100% nylon yarn, medium, worsted weight, .87oz/25g = approx 78yd/72m per ball, color #4603 Fellini Mix

(B) 9 hanks of Berroco Yarns' *Softwist*, 59% rayon/41% wool yarn, medium, worsted weight, 1.75oz/50g = approx 100yd/92m per hank, color #9455 Cool Red

fiesta

Have you ever been to
a South American bazaar,
with colorful hanging rugs,
pottery, and sweaters?
This easy-to-knit diagonal-rib
afghan will bring an open-air
feeling to your home.

SKILL LEVEL
Beginner

Finished Measurement

45 x 55"/114 x 140cm,

Yarn

Approx total: 1215 yd/1111m wool, medium weight yarn

Color A: 405yd/370m

Color B: 540yd/494m

Color C: 270yd/247m

Materials

Knitting needles: 6mm (Size 10 U.S.) *or size to obtain gauge*

Tapestry needle for weaving the ends

Large crochet hook for attaching fringe

Cardboard strip, 4"/10cm wide, for making the fringe

Gauge

14 sts = 4"/10cm in St st
Always take time to check your gauge.

Pattern Notes

There are three horizontal color panels of A, four of B, and two of C. Each color section is worked over 26 rows. The fringe is made of three colors, A, B, and C.

Pattern Stitch

FIESTA DIAGONAL RIB STITCH (CHART A)

Row 1 (RS): K3, *p3, k3; rep from* to end.

Row 2 (WS): P3, *k3, p3; rep from* to end.

Row 3: Rep row 1.

Row 4: K1, *p3, k3; rep from* to the last 2 sts, p2.

Row 5: K2, *p3, k3; rep from* to the last st, p1.

Rows 6 & 7: Rep row 4.

Row 8: Rep row 5.

Row 9: Rep row 4.

Row 10: K3, *p3, k3; rep from* to end.

Row 11: Rep row 2.

Row 12: Rep row 10.

Row 13: P2, *k3, p3; rep from* to last st, k1.

Row 14: P1, *k3, p3; rep from* to last 2 sts, k2.

Rows 15 & 16: Rep row 13.

Row 17: Rep row 14.

Row 18: Rep row 13.

Rep rows 1–18 for pat.

Chart A

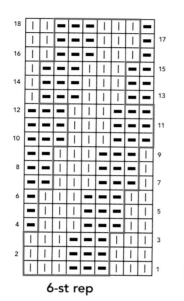

6-st rep

	K on RS, P on WS
▬	P on RS, K on WS

Afghan

With A, CO 165 stitches. *Work 26 rows of the pattern in A, 26 rows in B, 26 rows in C, 26 rows in B; repeat from * once more and end the work with 26 rows in A. Bind off all stitches.

Fringe

The general instructions for making fringe are on page 20. Using colors A, B, and C, make each fringe by wrapping the yarn 10 times around the width of the cardboard. Attach the fringes along one short edge of the afghan in the following color pat, *A, B, C, B, rep from* ending with A. Repeat on the other edge.

Design Tip

This afghan is a bright addition for any room. Teenage knitters will take to the simple stitches in the mixed variety of colors.

This afghan was knit with:

(A) 3 hanks of Manos del Uruguay's *Handspun Pure Wool (Kettle Dye)* 100% medium, worsted weight, 100g = approx 135yd/123m per hank, color #106

(B) 4 hanks of Manos del Uruguay's *Handspun Pure Wool (Kettle Dye)* 100% medium, worsted weight, 100g = approx 135yd/123m per hank, color #109

(C) 2 hanks of Manos del Uruguay's *Handspun Pure Wool (Kettle Dye)* 100% medium, worsted weight, 100g = approx 135yd/123m per hank, color #113

queen's treasure

This distinctive afghan reminds us of pennants flying majestically from the stone walls of a medieval castle. Each diamond is knit in soft shimmering yarn, then accented with gold emblems and tassels. This is the perfect afghan to make as a treasured gift for a favorite friend.

Finished Measurements

Afghan: 66 x 71"/168 x 180cm

Diamonds: 10 1/2 x 11"/ 27 x 28cm

Yarn

Approx total: 3534yd/3231m nylon, medium weight yarn

Color A: 1860yd/1701m in green

Color B: 558yd/510m in black

Color C: 279yd/255m in blue

Color D: 279yd/255m in yellow

Color E: 279yd/255m in red

Color F: 279yd/255m in orange

Color G: Approx total: 208yd/190m viscose/polyester blend, lightweight yarn in gold

Materials

Knitting needles: 4mm (Size 7 U.S.) *or size to obtain gauge*

Tapestry needle for sewing the seams and attaching the tassels

Crochet hook for attaching the tassels and making the emblems

Cardboard, 5"/12.7cm long, for making the tassels

Gauge

18 sts and 24 rows = 4"/10cm over St st using Color A.
Always take time to check your gauge.

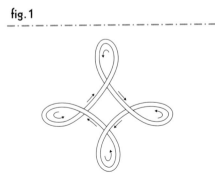

fig. 1

Pattern Note

The diamonds are reversible.

Special Abbreviations

Inc 1: Knit in front then in back of stitch.

Skp: Slip one stitch. Knit next stitch and pass the slip stitch over the knit stitch.

Sk2p: Slip one stitch, knit two stitches together. Pass the slipped stitch over two stitches knit together.

Pattern Stitch

DIAMONDS

Make 40 diamonds in A, 12 in B, 5 in C, D, E, and F for a total of 72 diamonds.

CO 3 sts. Knit one row.

Row 1: Inc 1, knit across.

Rep row 1 until there are 44 sts on RH ndls.

Row 44: Skp, knit across.

Rep row 44 until 3 sts remains on RH ndls.

Last row: Work sk2p. Pull yarn through remaining st. Cut.

Afghan

Using A, B, C, D, E, or F, seam the diamonds together according to the placement diagram.

Finishing

Weave the ends in.

Emblems

Make 12. Crochet a 14"/35.6cm chain (see page 21) using two strands of Color G held together. Using a slip stitch, attach the end of the crocheted chain to the beginning. Form this crocheted chain into four counter-clockwise loops, as shown in figure 1. Place each golden emblem in the center of the black diamonds and attach securely.

Tassels

Make 26. The general instructions for making tassels are on page 20. Using G, wrap the yarn 12 times around the width of the cardboard, then wrap the yarn to make the head, leaving a length of yarn for attachment. Trim the edges of each tassel. Attach the tassels to all 26 corners of the afghan.

Design Tip

When seaming the diamonds together, be sure to make each seam as tight as possible so the finished afghan will be secure.

Placement Diagram

◆ Color A (green)

◆ Color B (black)

◆ Color C (blue)

◆ Color D (yellow)

◆ Color E (red)

◆ Color F (orange)

This afghan was knit with:

(A) 20 balls of GGH Yarns' *Gala*, 100% nylon yarn, medium, worsted weight, 50g = approx 93yd/85m per ball, color #15

(B) 6 balls of GGH Yarns' *Gala*, 100% nylon yarn, medium, worsted weight, 50g = approx 93yd/85m per ball, color #7

(C) 3 balls of GGH Yarns' *Gala*, 100% nylon yarn, medium, worsted weight, 50g = approx 93yd/85m per ball, color #19

(D) 3 balls of GGH Yarns' *Gala*, 100% nylon yarn, medium, worsted weight, 50g = approx 93yd/85m per ball, color #17

(E) 3 balls of GGH Yarns' *Gala*, 100% nylon yarn, medium, worsted weight, 50g = approx 93yd/85m per ball, color #6

(F) 3 balls of GGH Yarns' *Gala*, 100% nylon yarn, medium, worsted weight, 50g = approx. 93yd/85m per ball, color #12

(G) 2 balls of Rowan Yarns' *Lurex Shimmer*, 80% viscose/20% polyester yarn, 25g = approx 104yd/95m per ball, color #332

lace and pearls

The lacy stitches in this afghan produce a delicate design that is offset by pearl-accented tassels. Two strands of silk thread are worked together to make a lightweight afghan that is guaranteed to shimmer in the moonlight.

Finished Measurements

50 x 60"/127 x 152cm, blocked

Yarn

Approx total: 4020yd/3674m silk, superfine weight yarn

Materials

Knitting needles: 4.5mm (Size 7 U.S.) *or size to obtain gauge*

Thirty-two 14mm white pearl beads

Tapestry needle for making the tassels and weaving in ends

Crochet hook for making and attaching the tassels

Gauge

20 sts and 20 rows=4"/10cm over St st using two strands tog
Always take time to check your gauge.

Pattern Note

The afghan is worked using two strands of yarn held together throughout.

Special Abbreviations

Skp: Slip one stitch. Knit next stitch and pass the slip stitch over the knit stitch.

Sk2p: Slip one stitch, knit two stitches together. Pass the slipped stitch over two stitches knit together.

Pattern Stitch

LACE AND PEARLS (CHART A)

Row 1 and all (WS): K1, p10, k1, *p3, k1, p10, k1 rep from * to end.

Rows 2 and 4: *P1, k10, p1, yo, sk2p, yo; rep from * end p1, k10, p1.

Rows 6, 10, and 14: *P1, k1, [yo, k1] 3 times, [skp] 3 times, p1, yo, sk2p, yo; rep from*, end p1, k1, [yo, k1] 3 times, [skp] 3 times, p1.

Rows 8 and 12: *P1, k1, [k1, yo] 3 times, [skp] 3 times, p1, yo, sk2p, yo; rep from*, end p1, k1, [k1, yo] 3 times, [skp] 3 times, p1.

Rows 16 and 18: Rep rows 2 and 4.

Rows 20, 24, and 28: *P1, [k2tog] 3 times, [k1, yo] 3 times, k1, p1, yo, k3tog, yo; rep from *, end p1, [k2tog] 3 times, [k1, yo] 3 times, k1, p1.

Rows 22 and 26: *P1, [k2tog] 3 times, [yo, k1] 3 times, k1, p1, yo, k3tog, yo; rep from * to end p1, [k2tog] 3 times, [yo, k1] 3 times, k1, p1.

Repeat rows 1–28 for pat.

Afghan

With two strands of yarn held together throughout, CO 243 stitches. Work in the pattern until the afghan measures approximately 60"/152cm from the beginning. Bind off all stitches.

Tassels

Make 32. Holding two strands of yarn together, crochet two, 7"/17.8cm chains, leaving 4"/10cm tails on both ends. Lay both crocheted chains in a cross fashion, one on top of the other. Fold both crocheted chains in half, bringing together the 4"/10cm tails and tie them together. These become the tail of the tassel. Place a 14mm pearl bead inside the crocheted chains above the tail, adjusting the chains evenly around the bead. With invisible thread, secure the top and sides of the four chains around the pearl bead so the bead sits securely on the tails. Cut a 6"/15.2cm piece of yarn, and use a tapestry needle to thread it around and through the head of the tassel. Repeat for the other tassels. Position 16 tassels evenly on one edge, and attach using a crochet hook. Do the same for the other edge. Trim the bottoms of the tassels if necessary.

Chart A

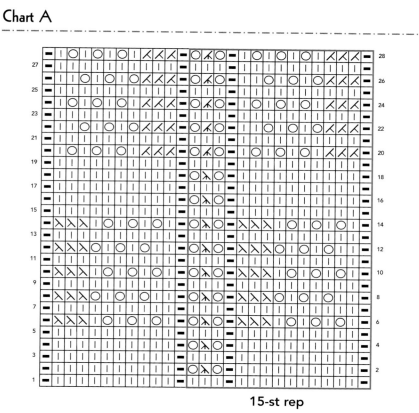

15-st rep

I	K on RS, P on WS
–	P on RS, K on WS
O	YO
⟋	K2tog
⟍	K3tog
λ	Skp
⋏	Sk2p

This afghan was knit with:

20 balls of Jaeger Yarns' *Silk*, 100% pure silk, superfine, fingering weight, 50g = approx 201yd/184m per ball, color #135 Silver Blue

sea breeze

Many happy days in our childhood were spent on the beach—picking up shells, dreaming of faraway places. Those memories inspired the color, texture, and pattern of this super-soft afghan. The easy shell pattern is knit by a repetition of single-strand and double-strand knitting, joining a strand of wool-blend yarn with a furry rayon-blend.

Finished Measurements

45 x 50"/114 x 127cm

Yarn

Color A: Approx total: 830yd/759m rayon blend, bulky weight yarn

Color B: Approx total: 2880yd/2632m wool blend lightweight yarn

Materials

Knitting needles: 5.5mm (Size 9 U.S.) *or size to obtain gauge*

Tapestry needle for weaving the ends

Gauge

14 sts and 20 rows = 4"/10cm over St st using strands of A and B held tog. *Always take time to check your gauge.*

Pattern Note

For Color AB, hold one strand of A and B together. For Color B, hold one strand of B. The afghan has 10 shell-pattern sections of color AB, and nine shell-pattern sections of color B.

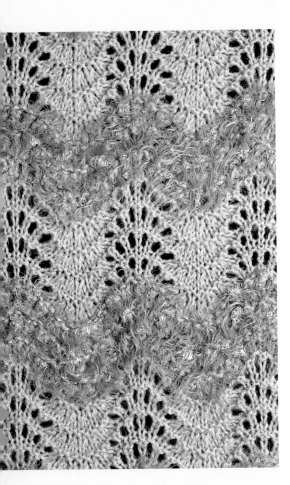

Pattern Stitch

SHELL STITCH (CHART A)

Row 1 (Right Side): Knit all sts.

Row 2 (Wrong Side): Purl.

Row 3: K1, *(k2tog) 3 times, (yo, k1) 6 times, (k2tog) 3 times; rep from * to last st, k1.

Row 4: Knit all sts.

Rep Rows 1–4 for pat.

Afghan

CO 200 stitches. *With AB, work rows 1–4 three times (one shell-pattern sec-

Design Tip

To make your work tangle free, roll the furry yarn (A) and the plain yarn (B) into one ball before you start to knit.

tion) from the pattern. Change to B, and work rows 1–4 four times. Repeat from * until 10 shell-pattern sections are completed in AB. Bind off all stitches.

Finishing

Weave the ends in.

Chart A

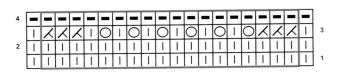

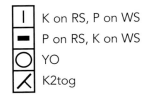

18 st rep

Ι	K on RS, P on WS
─	P on RS, K on WS
O	YO
⊼	K2tog

This afghan was knit with:

(A) 10 balls of GGH Yarns' *Fee*, 80% nylon/15% rayon/5% polyester yarn, bulky, chunky weight, 50g = approx 83yd/75m per ball, color #011

(B) 10 skeins of Stylecraft's *Pavlova*, 60% acrylic/20% wool/20% nylon yarn, light, DK weight, 100g = approx 288yd/263m per skein, color #3487 Hyacinth Blue

cross lane cables

Rib knit entwines with cross lane cables to become the central motif for this classic afghan. Its resemblance to a cable-knit sweater bears up in the afghan's comforting weight and welcoming warmth.

SKILL LEVEL
Intermediate

Finished Measurements

40 x 50"/102 x 127cm

Yarn

Approx total: 2024yd/1850m acrylic, medium weight yarn

Color A: 1771yd/1619m in copper

Color B: 253yd/231m in black

Materials

Knitting needles: 6.0 mm (Size 10 U.S.) *or size to obtain gauge*

Cable needle

Tapestry needle for weaving the ends

Large crochet hook for attaching the fringe

Cardboard strip, 5½"/14cm wide, for making the fringes

Gauge

16 sts and 20 rows = 4"/10cm over St st
Always take time to check your gauge.

Pattern Note

The afghan begins with a 13"/ 33cm rib section followed by cable pattern A, then a 4"/10cm rib section, then cable pattern B, and ends with a 13"/33cm rib section. Each of the cable patterns will be worked once. The tassels are made using A and B together.

Special Abbreviations

3-st right purl cable: Sl 1 st to cn and hold to back of work, k2, p1 from cn.

3-st left purl cable: Sl 2 sts to cn and hold to front of work, p1, k2 from cn.

4-st right twist: Sl 2 sts to cn and hold to back of work, k2, p2 from cn.

4-st left twist: Sl 2 sts to cn and hold to front of work, p2, k2 from cn.

4-st right cable: Sl 2 sts to cn and hold to back of work, k2, k2 from cn.

4-st left cable: Sl 2 sts to cn and hold to front of work, k2, k2 from cn.

Pattern Stitch

CROSS LANE CABLE A (CHART A)

Row 1(WS): K2 *p4, k4, repeat from * end last repeat with k2 instead of k4.

Rows 2, 6, and 10: P2, *4-st left cable, p4, 4-st right cable, p4, rep from *, end last repeat p2 instead of p4.

Row 3 and every other row: K the knit sts, p the purl sts.

Rows 4 and 8: P2, *k4, p4, rep from *, end last repeat p2 instead of p4.

Row 12: P1, *3-st right purl cable, 4-st left twist, 4-st right twist, 3-st left purl cable, p2, rep from *, end last repeat p1 instead of p2.

Row 14: P1, *k2, p3, 4-st right cable, p3, k2, p2, rep from *, end last repeat p1 instead of p2.

Row 16: P1, *3-st left purl cable, 4-st right twist, 4-st left twist, 3-st right purl cable, p2, rep from *, end last repeat p1 instead of p2.

Rows 18, 22, and 26: P2, *4-st right cable, p4, 4-st left cable, p4, rep from *, end last rep p2 instead of p4.

Rows 20 and 24: Rep row 4.

Row 28: P1, 3-st right purl cable, 3-st left purl cable, *p2, 3-st right purl cable, 4-st left twist, 4-st right twist, 3-st left purl cable, rep from *, end last rep p2, 3-st right purl cable, 3-st left purl cable, p1.

Row 30: P1, (k2, p2) twice, *k2, p3, 4-st left cable, p3, k2, p2, rep from *, end k2, p2, k2, p1.

Row 32: P1, 3-st left purl cable, 3-st right purl cable, *p2, 3-st left purl cable, 4-st right twist, 4-st left twist, 3-st right purl cable, rep from *, end last rep p2, 3-st left purl cable, 3-st right purl cable, p1.

Rows 33–43: Rep rows 1–11 once.

Work rows 1–43 once for cable pat A

CROSS LANE CABLE B (CHART B)

Row 1(WS): K2 *p4, k4* end last repeat with k2 instead of k4.

Rows 2, 6, and 10: P2, *4-st left cable, p4, 4-st right cable, p4, rep from *, end last repeat p2 instead of p4.

Row 3 and every other row: K the knit sts, p the purl sts.

Rows 4 and 8: P2, *k4, p4, rep from *, end last repeat p2 instead of p4.

Design Tip

Using the chart will make knitting this afghan easier.

Chart A

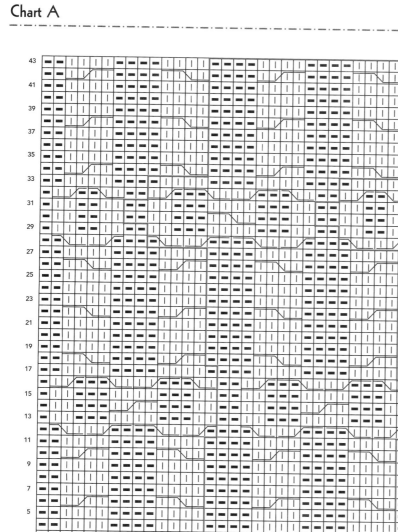

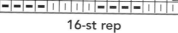

16-st rep

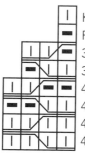

	K on RS, P on WS
	P on RS, K on WS
	3-st right purl cable
	3-st left purl cable
	4-st right twist
	4-st left twist
	4-st right cable
	4-st left cable

Chart B

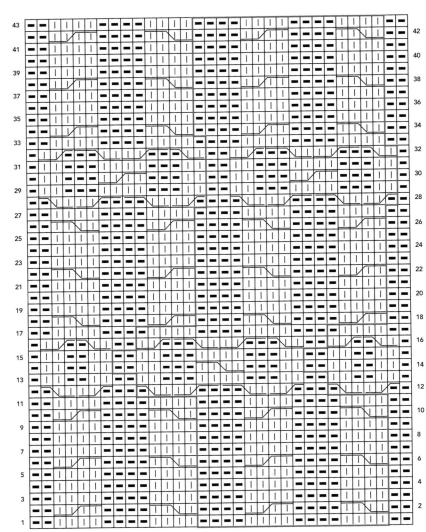

43
41
39
37
35
33
31
29
27
25
23
21
19
17
15
13
11
9
7
5
3
1

42
40
38
36
34
32
30
28
26
24
22
20
18
16
14
12
10
8
6
4
2

16-st rep

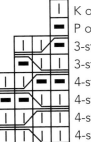

| | K on RS, P on WS
| ▬ | P on RS, K on WS
| | | ▬ | 3-st right purl cable
| ▬ | | | 3-st left purl cable
| | | ▬ ▬ | 4-st right twist
| ▬ ▬ | | | 4-st left twist
| | | | | | 4-st right cable
| | | | | | 4-st left cable

Row 12: P1, 3-st right purl cable, 3-st left purl cable, *p2, 3-st right purl cable, 4-st left twist, 4-st right twist, 3-st left purl cable, rep from *, end last rep p2, 3-st right purl cable, 3-st left purl cable, p1.

Row 14: P1, (k2, p2) twice, *k2, p3, 4-st left cable, p3, k2, p2, rep from *, end k2, p2, k2, p1.

Row 16: P1, 3-st left purl cable, 3-st right purl cable, *p2, 3-st left purl cable, 4-st right twist, 4-st left twist, 3-st right purl cable, rep from *, end last rep p2, 3-st left purl cable, 3-st right purl cable, p1.

Rows 18, 22, and 26: P2, *4-st right cable, p4, 4-st left cable, p4, rep from *, end last rep p2 instead of p4.

Rows 20 and 24: Rep row 4.

Row 28: P1, *3-st right purl cable, 4-st left twist, 4-st right twist, 3-st left purl cable, p2, rep from *, end last repeat p1 instead of p2.

Row 30: P1, *k2, p3, 4-st right cable, p3, k2, p2, rep from *, end last repeat p1 instead of p2.

Row 32: P1, *3-st left purl cable, 4-st right twist, 4-st left twist, 3-st right purl cable, p2, rep from *, end last repeat p1 instead of p2.

Rows 33–43: Rep rows 1–11 once.

Work rows 1–43 once for cable pat B.

RIB STITCH

Row 1: P2, *k4, p4, rep from *, end p2 instead of p4.

Row 2: K2, *p4, k4, rep from *, end k2 instead of k4.

Rep rows 1 and 2 for rib pat.

Afghan

With A, CO 168 stitches. Work two rows in the garter stitch. Keeping four stitches at the beginning and end of each row in the garter stitch throughout, work the rib stitch over 160 stitches for 13"/33cm. Work cable pattern A once. Work in rib for 4"/10cm. Work cable pattern B once. Work in rib for 13"/33cm. Work two rows in the garter stitch. Bind off all stitches.

Finishing

Weave the ends in. Block lightly.

Fringe

Make 44. The general instructions for making fringe are on page 20. With A and B together, wrap the yarns three times around the width of the cardboard strip. For each edge, attach 22 fringes directly below the knit rib stitches and the corners of the afghan. Trim the ends of the fringe.

This afghan was knit with:

(A) 7 skeins of Coats & Clark Yarn's *TLC*, 100% acrylic yarn, medium, worsted weight, 5oz/140g = approx 253yd/231m per skein, color #5289 Copper

(B) 1 skein of Coats & Clark Yarn's *TLC*, 100% acrylic yarn, medium, worsted weight, 5oz/140g = approx 253yd/231m per skein, color #5012 Black

cashmere earthtones

We love cables and wanted an afghan that included a unique way of creating them—and what better way than a horizontal cable pattern. Each square is knit with a splendid cashmere-blend yarn to make the completed afghan warm and luxuriously soft.

Finished Measurements

56 x 62"/ 142 x 157cm, blocked

Yarn

Approx total: 8768yd/8014m cashmere/extra fine merino blend, superfine yarn

Color A: 3836yd/3506m in brown

Color B: 3288yd/3005m in beige

Color C: 1644yd/1503m in ecru

Materials

Knitting needles: 4.5mm (Size 7 U.S.) or *size to obtain gauge*

Cable needle

Tapestry needle for sewing the seams

Large crochet hook for attaching the tassels

Cardboard strip, 7"/18cm wide, for making the tassels

Gauge

20 sts and 26 rows = 4"/10cm in St st using two strands
Always take time to check your gauge.

Pattern Note

Since the yarn is very fine, two strands of the same color are held throughout in knitting the cable blocks. There will be eight cable blocks in eight rows for a total of 64 cable blocks in the afghan.

Special Abbreviations

6-st right cable: Slip 3 stitches to the cable needle and hold to back of work, k3, k3 from the cable needle.

6-st left cable: Slip 3 stitches to the cable needle and hold to front of work, k3, k3 from cn.

Skp: Slip one stitch. Knit the next stitch and pass the slipped stitch over the knit stitch.

Pattern Stitch

CASHMERE EARTHTONES CABLE PATTERN A (CHART A)

Row 1: K25, k2tog, p2, k6, p2, yo, k1.

Row 2 (WS) and every other row: K the knit sts, purl the purl sts and the yo from previous row.

Row 3: K24, k2tog, p2, k6, p2, yo, k2.

Row 5: K23, k2tog, p2, 6-st right cable, p2, yo, k3.

Row 7: K22, k2tog, p2, k6, p2, yo, k4.

Row 9: K21, k2tog, p2, k6, p2, yo, k5.

Row 11: K20, k2tog, p2, k6, p2, yo, k6.

Row 13: K19, k2tog, p2, 6-st right cable, p2, yo, k7.

Row 15: K18, k2tog, p2, k6, p2, yo, k8.

Row 17: K17, k2tog, p2, k6, p2, yo, k9.

Row 19: K16, k2tog, p2, k6, p2, yo, k10.

Row 21: K15, k2tog, p2, 6-st right cable, p2, yo, k11.

Row 23: K14, k2tog, p2, k6, p2, yo, k12.

Row 25: K13, k2tog, p2, k6, p2, yo, k13.

Row 27: K12, k2tog, p2, k6, p2, yo, k14.

Row 29: K11, k2tog, p2, 6-st right cable, p2, yo, k15.

Row 31: K10, k2tog, p2, k6, p2, yo, k16.

Row 33: K9, k2tog, p2, k6, p2, yo, k17.

Row 35: K8, k2tog, p2, k6, p2, yo, k18.

Row 37: K7, k2tog, p2, 6-st right cable, p2, yo, k19.

Row 39: K6, k2tog, p2, k6, p2, yo, k20.

Row 41: K5, k2tog, p2, k6, p2, yo, k21.

Row 43: K4, k2tog, p2, k6, p2, yo, k22.

Row 45: K3, k2tog, p2, 6-st right cable, p2, yo, k23.

Row 47: K2, k2tog, p2, k6, p2, yo, k24.

Row 49: K1, k2tog, p2, k6, p2, yo, k25.

Row 50: Work Row 2.

Work rows 1–50 once for cable pat A.

CASHMERE EARTHTONES CABLE PATTERN B (CHART B)

Row 1: K1, yo, p2, k6, p2, skp, k25.

Row 2 (WS) and every other row: Knit the k sts, Purl the p sts and the yo from previous row.

Row 3: K2, yo, p2, k6, p2, skp, k24.

Row 5: K3, yo, p2, 6-st left cable, p2, skp, k23.

Row 7: K4, yo, p2, k6, p2, skp, k22.

Row 9: K5, yo, p2, k6, p2, skp, k21.

Row 11: K6, yo, p2, k6, p2, skp, k20.

Row 13: K7, yo, p2, 6-st left cable, p2, skp, k19.

Row 15: K8, yo, p2, k6, p2, skp, k18.

Row 17: K9, yo, p2, k6, p2, skp, k17.

Row 19: K10, yo, p2, k6, p2, skp, k16.

Row 21: K11, yo, p2, 6-st left cable, p2, skp, k15.

Row 23: K12, yo, p2, k6, p2, skp, k14.

Row 25: K13, yo, p2, k6, p2, skp, k13.

Row 27: K14, yo, p2, k6, p2, skp, k12.

Row 29: K15, yo, p2, 6-st left cable, p2, skp, k11.

Row 31: K16, yo, p2, k6, p2, skp, k10.

Row 33: K17, yo, p2, k6, p2, skp, k9.

Row 35: K18, yo, p2, k6, p2, skp, k8.

Row 37: K19, yo, p2, 6-st left cable, p2, skp, k7.

Row 39: K20, yo, p2, k6, p2, skp, k6.

Row 41: K21, yo, p2, k6, p2, skp, k5.

Row 43: K22, yo, p2, k6, p2, skp, k4.

Row 45: K23, yo, p2, 6-st left cable, p2, skp, k3.

Row 47: K24, yo, p2, k6, p2, skp, k2.

Row 49: K25, yo, p2, k6, p2, skp, k1.

Row 50: Work row 2.

Work rows 1–50 once for cable pat B.

Afghan

Make 64 cable squares.

CABLE BLOCK A

Make six in A, eight in B, four in C. Cast on 38 sts. Work cable pat B. Bind off.

CABLE BLOCK B

Make six in A, eight in B, four in C. Cast on 38 sts. Work cable pat A. Bind off.

CABLE BLOCK C

Make two in A, one in B. Cast on 42 sts. Work four sts in garter st, work 38 sts over cable pat B. Cont in pat as est. Bind off.

CABLE BLOCK D

Make two in A, one in B. Cast on 42 sts. Work four sts in garter st, work 38 sts over cable pat A. Cont in pat as est. Bind off.

Chart A

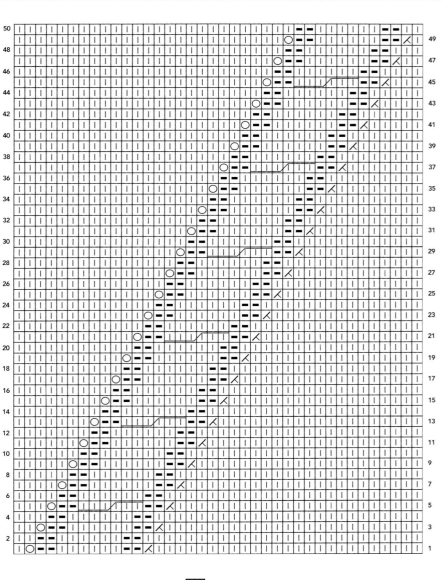

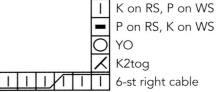

	K on RS, P on WS
-	P on RS, K on WS
O	YO
⋋	K2tog
	6-st right cable

Chart B

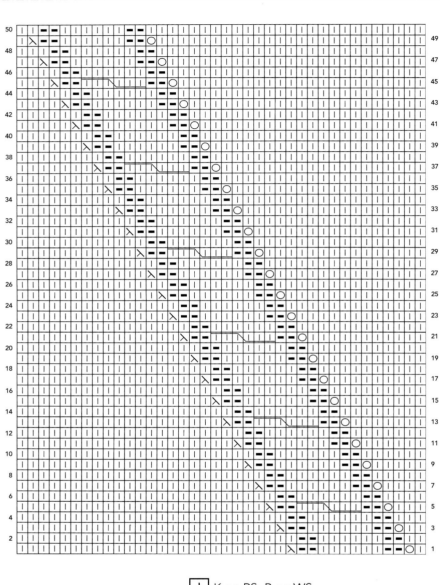

CABLE BLOCK E

Make two in A, one in B. Cast on 42 sts. Work 38 sts over cable pat B, work four sts in garter st. Cont in pat as est. Bind off.

CABLE BLOCK F

Make two in A, one in B. Cast on 42 sts. Work 38 sts over cable pat A, work four sts in garter st. Cont in pat as est. Bind off.

CABLE BLOCK G

Make two in A, one in B. Cast on 38 sts. Work cable pat B. Work four rows in garter st. Bind off.

CABLE BLOCK H

Make two in A, one in B. Cast on 38 sts. Work cable pat A. Work four rows in garter st. Bind off.

CABLE BLOCK I

Make two in A, one in B. Cast on 38 sts. Work four rows in garter st. Work cable pat B. Bind off.

CABLE BLOCK J

Make two in A, one in B. Cast on 38 sts. Work four rows in garter st. Work cable pat A. Bind off.

CABLE BLOCK K

Make one in C. Cast on 42 sts. Work four rows in garter st. Work cable pat B over 38 sts, work four sts in garter st. Cont in pat as est. Bind off.

	K on RS, P on WS
▬	P on RS, K on WS
O	YO
⋋	Skp

6-st left cable

Placement Diagream

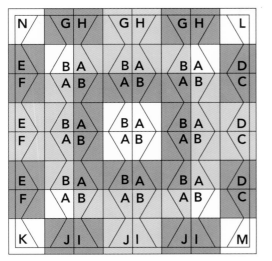
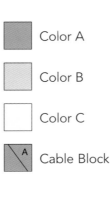

- Color A
- Color B
- Color C
- A Cable Block

CABLE BLOCK L

Make one in C. Cast on 42 sts. Work four sts in garter st, work cable pat B over 38 sts. Cont in pat as est. Work four rows in garter st. Bind off.

CABLE BLOCK M

Make one in C. Cast on 42 sts. Work four rows in garter st. Work four sts in garter st, work cable pat A over 38 sts. Cont in pat as est. Bind off.

CABLE BLOCK N

Make one in C. Cast on 42 sts. Work cable pat A over 38 sts, work four sts in garter sts. Cont in pat as est. Work four rows in garter st. Bind off.

Joining Cable Blocks

With A, B, or C, seam the cable blocks together according to the placement diagram.

Finishing

Weave the ends in. Block lightly.

Tassels

Make four. The general instructions for making tassels are on page 20. Using A, B, and C, wrap the yarn 15 times around the width of the cardboard strip. Trim the edges of each tassel. Attach the tassels to all four corners of the afghan.

Design Tip

Since cashmere is quite expensive, try to conserve as much yarn as possible by knitting small amounts of leftover yarn and attaching it to a new ball.

This project was knit with:

(A) 28 balls of Jaeger Handknit Yarns' *Cashmina*, 80% cashmere/ 20% extra fine merino, superfine, fingering weight, 25g = approx 137yd/125m per ball, color #032 Moutarde

(B) 24 balls of Jaeger Handknit Yarns' *Cashmina*, 80% cashmere/ 20% extra fine merino, superfine, fingering weight, 25g = approx 137yd/125m per ball, color #031 Beige

(C) 12 balls of Jaeger Handknit Yarns' *Cashmina*, 80% cashmere/ 20% extra fine merino, superfine, fingering weight, 25g = approx 137yd/125m per ball, color #030 Ecru

bold and beautiful

You can comfortably knit this easy slip-stitch afghan in a week. The bright colors contrast with the black velvet in a chenille yarn that is irresistibly soft.

Finished Measurements

43 x 50"/109 x 127cm

Yarn

Approx total: 1000yd/914m acrylic/rayon blend, bulky weight yarn

Color A: 400yd/366m in black

Color B: 100yd/91m in scarlet

Color C: 100yd/91m in turquoise

Color D: 100yd/91m in hot pink

Color E: 100yd/91m in dark purple

Color F: 100yd/91m in olive

Color G: 100yd/91m in royal blue

Materials

Knitting needles: 6mm (Size 10 U.S.) *or size to obtain gauge*

Tapestry needle for weaving the ends

Large crochet hook for attaching the fringe

Cardboard strip, 5"/12.7cm wide, for making the fringe

Gauge

8 sts and 16 rows = 4"/10cm over St st
Always take time to check your gauge.

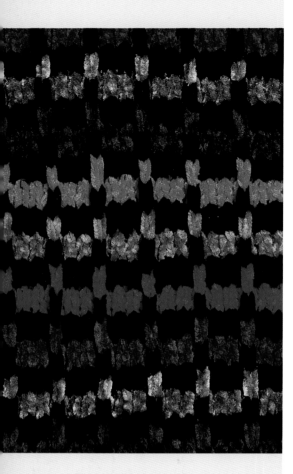

Pattern Note

When working from the chart, work the stitches in the colors shown.

Special Abbreviations

Sl 1 wyif: Slip 1 with yarn in front.

Sl 1 wyib: Slip 1 with yarn in back.

Pattern Stitch

BOLD AND BEAUTIFUL STITCH (CHART A)

Row 1 (WS): With A, purl.

Rows 2 and 4: With B, k3, *sl 1 wyib, k3; rep from * to end.

Row 3: With B, p3, *sl 1 wyif, p3; rep from * to end.

Row 5: With B, purl.

Rows 6, 7, 8, and 9: With A, rep rows 2, 3, 4, and 5.

Rows 10, 11, 12, and 13: With C, rep rows 2, 3, 4, and 5.

Rows 14, 15, 16, and 17: With A, rep rows 2, 3, 4, and 5.

Rows 18, 19, 20, and 21: With D, rep rows 2, 3, 4, and 5.

Rows 22, 23, 24, and 25: With A, rep rows 2, 3, 4, and 5.

Rows 26, 27, 28, and 29: With E, rep rows 2, 3, 4, and 5.

Rows 30, 31, 32, and 33: With A, rep rows 2, 3, 4, and 5.

Rows 34, 35, 36, and 37: With F, rep rows 2, 3, 4, and 5.

Rows 38, 39, 40, and 41: With A, rep rows 2, 3, 4, and 5.

Rows 42, 43, 44, and 45: With G, rep rows 2, 3, 4, and 5.

Rows 46, 47, and 48: With A, rep rows 2, 3, and 4.

Rep rows 1–48 for pat.

Chart A

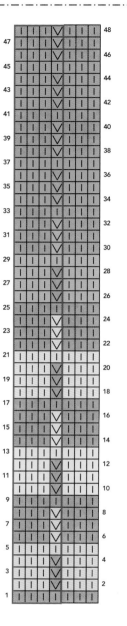

 Knit on RS, purl on WS

Sl 1 wyib on RS; sl 1 wyif on WS

Work sts in the displayed color

Afghan

With A, CO 95 stitches. Work rows
1–48 four times, then repeat rows
1–9 once more from the pattern.
Bind off all stitches.

Design Tip

To create your own signature afghan,
you can substitute the pattern color
combination with your own.

Finishing

Weave the ends in.

Fringe

Make enough fringe to attach across the
two edges of the afghan. The general
instructions for making fringe are on
page 20. Using A, B, C, D, E, F, and G,
make fringe by wrapping the yarn three
times around the width of the cardboard
strip. Attach the fringe to one edge in the
following alternating pattern, A, B, A, C,
A, D, A, E, A, F, A, G. Repeat for the other
edge and trim the ends of the fringe.

This afghan was knit with:

(A) 4 skeins of Lion Brand Yarn's
Chenille Thick & Quick, 91% acrylic/
9% rayon, super bulky, bulky yarn,
5oz/140g = approx 100yd/91m per
skein, color #153 Black

(B) 1 skein of Lion Brand Yarn's
Chenille Thick & Quick, 91% acrylic/
9% rayon, super bulky, bulky yarn,
5 oz/140g = approx 100yd/91m per
skein, color #113 Scarlet

(C) 1 skein of Lion Brand Yarn's
Chenille Thick & Quick, 91% acrylic/
9% rayon, super bulky, bulky yarn,
5 oz/140g = approx 100yd/91m per
skein, color #148 Turquoise

(D) 1 skein of Lion Brand Yarn's
Chenille Thick & Quick, 91% acrylic/
9% rayon, super bulky, bulky yarn,
5 oz/140g= approx 100yd/91m per
skein, color #195 Hot Pink

(E) 1 skein of Lion Brand Yarn's
Chenille Thick & Quick, 91% acrylic/
9% rayon, super bulky, bulky yarn,
5oz/140g = approx 100yd/91m per
skein, color #146 Dark Purple

(F) 1 skein of Lion Brand Yarn's
Chenille Thick & Quick, 91% acrylic/
9% rayon, super bulky, bulky yarn,
5oz/140g = approx 100yd/91m per
skein, color #132 Olive

(G) 1 skein of Lion Brand Yarn's
Chenille Thick & Quick, 91% acrylic/
9% rayon, super bulky, bulky yarn,
5oz/140g = approx 100yd/91m per
skein, color #109 Royal Blue

stormy weather

Stranded on a stormy night? This afghan will wrap you in its warmth. The nine classic cable patterns are surprisingly quick to knit, and create a rugged look. Men especially appreciate its bold pattern and subtle color.

Finished Measurements

45 x 52"/114 x 132cm, blocked

Yarn

Approx total: 1300yds/1189m wool, medium weight yarn

Materials

Knitting needles: 6mm (Size 10 U.S.) *or size to obtain gauge*

Cable needle

Tapestry needle for sewing the seams and weaving the ends

Large crochet hook for attaching the fringe

Cardboard strip, 5"/12.7cm wide, for making the fringe

Gauge

15 sts = 4"/10cm over St st
Always take time to check your gauge.

Pattern Note

There are four large and four small side panels plus one central panel. The placement diagram at the end of this pattern will show you how to assemble the panels for seaming.

Special Abbreviations

Make 1 (M1): Purl into the horizontal strand before the next stitch.

9-st left purl twist: Sl 5 sts to cn and hold in front of work, k4, p1 from cn; then k4 from cn.

2-st right purl twist: Sl 1 st to cn and hold to back of work, k1, p1 from cn.

2-st left purl twist: Sl 1 st to cn and hold to front of work, p1, k1 from cn.

3-st right purl cable: Sl 1 st to cn and hold to back of work, k2, p1, from cn.

3-st left purl cable: Sl 2 sts to cn and hold to front of work, p1, k2 from cn.

3-st right cable: Sl 1 st to cn and hold to back of work, k2, k1 from cn.

3-st left cable: Sl 2 sts to cn and hold to front of work, k1, k2 from cn.

4-st right cable: Sl 2 sts to cn and hold to back of work, k2, k2 from cn.

4-st left cable: Sl 2 sts to cn and hold to front of work, k2, k2 from cn.

5-st right cable: Sl 3 sts to cn and hold to back of work, k2, sl purl st from cn to LH needle and purl it, k2 from cn.

6-st right cable: Sl 3 sts to cn and hold to back of work, k3, k3 from cn.

6-st left cable: Sl 3 sts to cn and hold to front of work, k3, k3 from cn.

12-st left cable: Sl 6 sts to cn and hold to front of work, k6, k6 from cn.

12-st right cable: Sl 6 sts to cn and hold to back of work, k6, k6 from cn.

Rope-st left cable: Sl 8 sts to cn and hold to front of work, k4, and then sl the 2nd 4sts from cn to LH needle. Then work them as foll: k4, k4 from cn.

Rope-st right cable: Sl 8 sts to cn and hold to back of work, k4, and then sl the 2nd 4sts from cn to LH needle. Then work them as foll: k4, k4 from cn.

Pattern Stitch

CENTRAL PANEL (CHART A)
(make 1)

Cast on 49 sts.

Row 1 (RS): (P2, k4) 4 times, p1, (k4, p2) 4 times.

Rows 2, 4, 6, and 8: Knit the k sts, purl the p sts.

Row 3: (P2, 4-st left cable, p2, k4) twice, p1, (k4, p2, 4-st right cable, p2) twice.

Row 5: Rep row 1.

Row 7: P2, 4-st left cable, p2, k4, p2, 4-st left cable, p2, work 9-st left purl twist, p2, 4-st right cable, p2, k4, p2, 4-st right cable, p2.

Row 9: P2, k4, p2, *M1, (k4, p2) twice, k4, M1*, p1, rep from * to * once, p2, k4, p2.

Row 10: K2, p4, *k3, p4, (k2, p4) twice*, rep from * to * once, k3, p4, k2.

Row 11: P2, 4-st left cable, p3, M1, k4, p2tog, 4-st left cable, p2tog, k4, M1, p3, M1, k4, p2tog, 4-st right cable, p2tog, k4, M1, p3, 4-st right cable, p2.

Row 12: K2, p4, k4, *(p4, k1) twice, p4 *, k5, rep from * to * once, k4, p4, k2.

Row 13: P2, k4, p4, *M1, k3, skp, k4, k2tog, k3, M1 *, p5, rep from * to * once, p4, k4, p2.

Central Panel (Chart A)

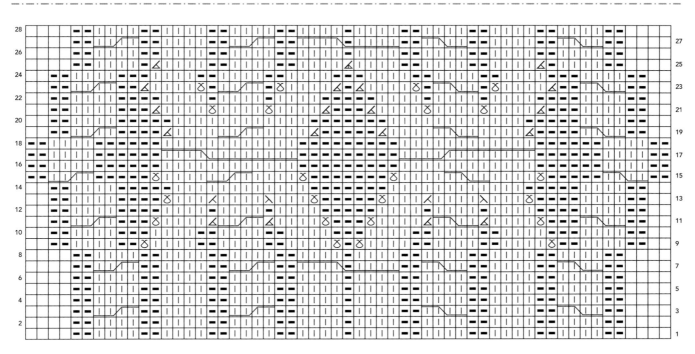

Row 14: K2, p4, k5, p12, k7, p12, k5, p4, k2.

Row 15: P2, 4-st left cable, p5, M1, k4, 4-st left cable, k4, M1, p7, M1, k4, 4-st right cable, k4, M1, p5, 4-st right cable, p2.

Row 16: K2, p4, k6, p12, k9, p12, k6, p4, k2.

Row 17: P2, k4, p6, Rope-st right cable, p9, Rope-st left cable, p6, k4, p2.

Row 18, 20, 22, and 24: Repeat rows 16, 14, 12, and 10.

Row 19: P2, 4-st left cable, p4, p2tog, k4, 4-st left cable, k4, p2tog, p5, p2tog, k4, 4-st right cable, k4, p2tog, p4, 4-st right cable, p2.

Row 21: P2, k4, p3, *p2tog, (k4, M1) twice, k4, p2tog, p3, rep from* once, k4, p2.

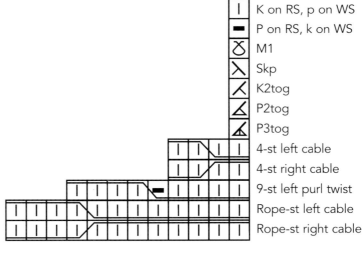

	K on RS, p on WS
▬	P on RS, k on WS
⊗	M1
⟍	Skp
⟋	K2tog
◺	P2tog
◺	P3tog
	4-st left cable
	4-st right cable
	9-st left purl twist
	Rope-st left cable
	Rope-st right cable

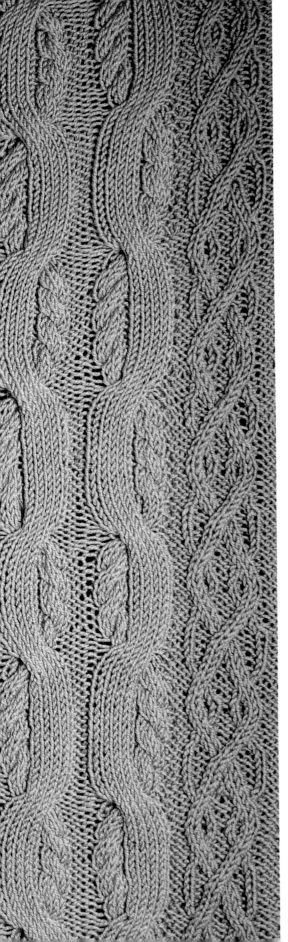

Large Side Panel (Chart B)

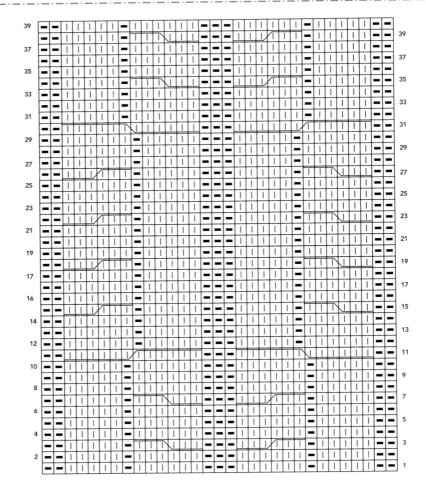

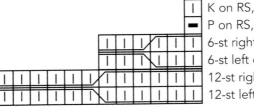

	K on RS, P on WS
	P on RS, K on WS
	6-st right cable
	6-st left cable
	12-st right cable
	12-st left cable

Row 23: P2, 4-st left cable, p2, p2tog, k4, M1, p1, 4-st left cable, p1, M1, k4, p2tog, p1, p2tog, k4, M1, p1, 4-st right cable, p1, M1, k4, p2tog, p2, 4-st right cable, p2.

Row 25: P2, k4, p1, p2tog, *(k4, p2) twice, k4 *, p3 tog, rep from * to * once, p2tog, p1, k4, p2.

Row 26: Rep row 2.

Row 27: Rep row 7.

Row 28: Rep row 2.

Repeat rows 1–28 for the Central Cable until 50". Bind off.

LARGE SIDE PANEL (CHART B) (Make 4)

Cast on 31 sts

Row 1 (RS): P2, k5, p1, k6, p3, k6, p1, k5, p2.

Row 2: K2, p5, k1, p6, k3, p6, k1, p5, k2.

Row 3: P2, k5, p1, 6-st right cable, p3, 6-st left cable, p1, k5, p2.

Row 4: Rep row 2.

Rows 5, 6, 7, and 8: Rep rows 1, 2, 3, and 4.

Row 9: Rep row 1.

Row 10: Rep row 2.

Row 11: P2, 12-st left cable, p3, 12-st right cable, p2.

Row 12: K2, p6, k1, p5, k3, p5, k1, p6, k2.

Row 13: P2, k6, p1, k5, p3, k5, p1, k6, p2.

Row 14: Rep row 12.

Row 15: P2, 6-st left cable, p1, k5, p3, k5, p1, 6-st right cable, p2.

Row 16: Rep row 12.

Rows 17–28: Rep rows 13–16 three times.

Row 29: Rep row 13.

Row 30: Rep row 14.

Row 31: P2, 12-st right cable, p3, 12-st left cable, p2.

Row 32: Rep row 2.

Rows 33–40: Rep Rows 1–4 twice.

Repeat rows 1–40 for the Large Side Panel until it measures 50"/127cm. Bind off.

SMALL SIDE PANEL (CHART C) (Make 4)

CO 15 sts.

Row 1 (WS): K2, p1, k2, p2, k1, p2, k2, p1, k2.

Row 2: P2, k1, p2, 5-st right cable, p2, k1, p2.

Row 3: Rep row 1.

Row 4: P2, 2-st left purl twist, 3-st right purl cable, p1, 3-st left purl cable, 2-st right purl twist, p2.

Row 5 and 7: [K3, p3] twice, k3.

Row 6: P3, 3-st right cable, p3, 3-st left cable, p3.

Row 8: P2, 3-st right purl cable, 2-st left purl twist, p1, 2-st right purl twist, 3-st left purl cable, p2.

Rows 9 and 11: K2, p2, k2, p1, k1, p1, k2, p2, k2.

Row 10: P2, k2, p2, k1, p1, k1, p2, k2, p2.

Row 12: P2, 3-st left purl cable, 2-st right purl twist, p1, 2-st left purl twist, 3-st right purl cable, p2.

Rows 13 and 15: Rep rows 5 and 7.

Row 14: P3, 3-st left cable, p3, 3-st right cable, p3.

Row 16: P2, 2-st right purl twist, 3-st left purl cable, p1, 3-st right purl cable, 2-st left purl twist, p2.

Repeat rows 1–16 for the Small Side Panel until 50". Bind off.

Finishing

With A, seam the panels together according to the placement diagram using the mattress stitch. Block the afghan.

Fringe

Make enough fringes to attach across the two edges of the afghan. The general instructions for making fringe are on page 20. Wrap the yarn four times around the width of the cardboard strip. Attach the fringe to the edges, spacing them ¼"/6mm apart, and trim the ends of the fringe.

Design Tip

In order to keep the texture of the cable, make sure that you don't flatten or stretch the cables when the afghan is wet or being blocked.

Small Side Panel (Chart C)

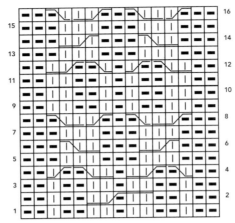

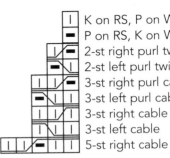

I	K on RS, P on WS
▬	P on RS, K on WS
	2-st right purl twist
	2-st left purl twist
	3-st right purl cable
	3-st left purl cable
	3-st right cable
	3-st left cable
	5-st right cable

Placement Chart

Small Side Panel	Large Side Panel	Small Side Panel	Large Side Panel	Center Panel	Large Side Panel	Small Side Panel	Large Side Panel	Small Side Panel

This afghan was knit with:

20 balls of Classic Elite Yarn's *Bazic Wool*, 100% superwash wool yarn, medium, worsted weight, 50g = approx 65 yds/59m per ball, color #2945

days~gone~by garden

Sometimes no design will do but an old-fashioned one, reminding us of days gone by and the sweet stories we used to hear. This afghan is a collection of spring-colored flowers embroidered on traditional basket-stitch squares. It's a perfect throw when you're in front of the fire dreaming of spring.

SKILL LEVEL
Intermediate

Finished Measurements

52 x 50"/132 x 127cm

Yarn

Approx total: 3132yd/2864m acrylic, worsted weight yarn

Color A: 2712yd/2480m in pale yellow

Color B: 70yd/64m in light blue

Color C: 70yd/64m in light mint

Color D: 70yd/64m in light raspberry

Color E: 70yd/64m in country rose

Color F: 70yd/64m in pale plum

Color G: 70yd/64m in lavender

Materials

Knitting needles: 6.0mm (Size 10 U.S.) *or size to obtain gauge*

Stitch markers

Tapestry needle for sewing the seams, gathering, and attaching the flowers

Gauge

16 sts and 20 rows = 4"/10cm over St st

Always take time to check your gauge.

Pattern Note

The flower has six leaves in the color combination of B and C [B, C, B, C, B, C] D and E, and F and G. For Panels C and D, place a marker between the border stitches and the pattern.

Special Abbreviations

Skp: Slip one stitch. Knit next stitch and pass the slip stitch over the knit stitch.

Make 1 (M1): Knit into the horizontal strand before the next stitch.

Pattern Stitch

BASKET STITCH (CHART A)

Row 1 (RS): K11, p2, k2, p2, k11.

Row 2: P1, k8, [p2, k2] twice, p2, k8, p1.

Row 3: K1, p8, [k2, p2] twice, k2, p8, k1.

Row 4: P11, k2, p2, k2, p11.

Rep rows 1–4 once more.

Row 9: Knit across.

Row 10: [P2, k2] twice, p12, [k2, p2] twice.

Row 11: [K2, p2] twice, k2, p8, [k2, p2] twice, k2.

Row 12: [P2, k2] twice, p2, k8, [p2, k2] twice, p2.

Row 13: [K2, p2] twice, k12, [p2, k2] twice.

Rep rows 10–13 once more.

Row 18: Purl across.

Rows 19–27: Rep rows 1–9.

Work rows 1–27 once for pat.

LEAF STITCH (CHART B)

Row 1 (RS): K3.

Row 2: Purl across.

Row 3: K1, [M1, k1] twice (5 sts).

Row 4: Purl across.

Row 5: K1, M1, k3, M1, k1 (7 sts).

Row 6: Purl across.

Row 7: K1, M1, k5, M1, k1 (9 sts).

Row 8: Purl across.

Row 9: Skp, k5, k2tog (7 sts).

Row 10: [Sl 1, p1, psso], p3, p2tog (5 sts).

Leave 5 sts on needle.

Chart A

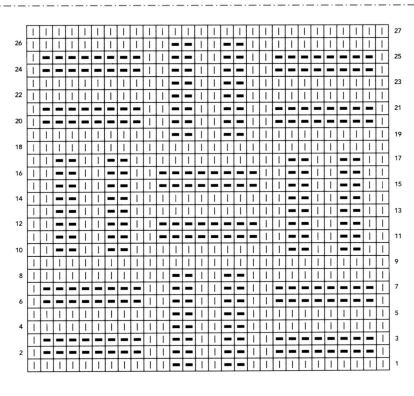

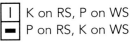

| | K on RS, P on WS |
| | P on RS, K on WS |

Chart B

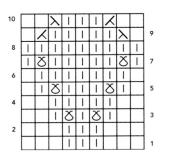

	K on RS, P on WS
-	P on RS, K on WS
⟋	K2tog on RS, p2tog on WS
⟍	Skp on RS, [sl 1, p1, psso] on WS
⊗	M1

Afghan Panels

PANEL A

Make two. With A, CO 28 sts. Knit four rows. *Work basket pat once. Knit five rows. Work St st for 27 rows. Knit five rows. Rep from* three more times. Work basket pat. Knit four rows. Bind off.

PANEL B

Make three. With A, CO 28 sts. Knit four rows. *Work St st for 27 rows. Knit five rows. Work basket pat once. Knit five rows. Rep from* three more times. Work St st for 27 rows. Knit four rows. Bind off.

PANEL C

Make one. With A, CO 32 sts. Work as for Panel A, keeping four sts left of pattern in garter sts throughout to create a left border. Bind off.

PANEL D

Make one.With A, CO 32 sts. Work as for Panel A, keeping four sts right of pattern in garter st throughout to create a right border. Bind off.

Joining Panels

With A, seam the panels together according to the placement diagram using the mattress stitch.

Leaf Stitch

Make 30 in B, C, D, and E, and 33 in F and G.

Cast on three sts. Work the leaf stitch, keeping remaining five sts on needle or cn needle.

Placement Diagram

Legend:
- Basket Pattern
- Blue-Green Flower
- Plum-Lavender Flower
- Raspberry Flower

| Panel C | Panel B | Panel A | Panel B | Panel A | Panel B | Panel D |

This afghan was knit with:

(A) 6 skeins of Red Heart Yarn's *Super Saver*, 100% acrylic yarn, medium, worsted weight, 8oz/225g = approx 452yd/413m per skein, color #0322 Pale Yellow

(B) 1 skein of Red Heart Yarn's *Super Saver*, 100% acrylic yarn, medium, worsted weight, 8oz/225g = approx 452yd/413m per skein, color #0381 Light Blue

(C) 1 skein of Red Heart Yarn's *Super Saver*, 100% acrylic yarn, medium, worsted weight, 8oz/225g = approx 452yd/413m per skein, color #0364 Light Mint

(D) 1 skein of Red Heart Yarn's *Super Saver*, 100% acrylic yarn, medium, worsted weight, 8oz/225g = approx 452yd/413m per skein, color #0774 Light Raspberry

(E) 1 skein of Red Heart Yarn's *Super Saver*, 100% acrylic yarn, medium, worsted weight, 8oz/225g = approx 452yd/413m per skein, color #0374 Country Rose

(F) 1 skein of Red Heart Yarn's *Super Saver*, 100% acrylic yarn, medium, worsted weight, 8oz/225g = approx 452yd/413m per skein, color #0579 Pale Plum

(G) 1 skein of Red Heart Yarn's *Super Saver*, 100% acrylic yarn, medium, worsted weight, 8oz/225g = approx 452yd/413m per skein, color #0358 Lavender

Flower Assembly

Make 10 flowers in B and C, D and E, and 11 in F and G. For a total of 31 flowers.

On one needle, keep leaves in the following order B, C, B, C, B, C. K2tog across all 30 sts on needle. Leaving 10"/25cm tail, cut yarn. Thread tapestry needle with cut tail and pull through 15 sts, gathering all six petals together. Tighten the petals and fasten securely to afghan according to placement diagram. Rep for remaining B and C, D and E, and F and G combination.

French Knot

The general instructions for the French knot are on page 17. Stitch a French knot in the center of each flower.

Finishing

Weave the ends in.

Design Tip

The flowers can be made with leftover yarn.

glamour

This sophisticated red-and-black afghan is composed of 80 knitted parallelograms stitched together using two sparkling metallic-blend yarns. This easy take-along project will add an extra touch of glamour to any room.

SKILL LEVEL
Easy

Finished Measurements

45 x 58"/114 x147cm

Yarn

Approx total: 2255yd/2062m viscose/metal blend, medium weight yarn

Color A: 1127yd/1031m in red

Color B: 1127yd/1031m in black

Materials

Knitting needles: 5.5mm (Size 9 U.S.) *or size to obtain gauge*

Tapestry needle for sewing the seams and weaving the ends

Large crochet hook for attaching the fringe

Cardboard strip, 5"/12.7cm wide, for making the fringe

Gauge

16 sts = 4"/10cm over St st
Always take time to check your gauge.

Pattern Note

The afghan is made of 80 parallelograms that are pieced together in 10 rows of eight each. Each parallelogram measures 6 x 5"/ 15.2 x 12.7cm

Special Abbreviations

Inc 1: Knit in front then in back of the stitch.

Skp: Slip one stitch. Knit the next stitch and pass the slip stitch over the knit stitch.

Sk2p: Slip one stitch, knit two stitches together. Pass the slipped stitch over two stitches knit together.

Design Tip

Since this is a large afghan, it's better to purchase the yarn in cones.

Pattern Stitch

· PARALLELOGRAMS

Row 1 (RS): With A, CO 3 sts.

Row 2: With A, purl.

Row 3: With A, inc 1, knit across, inc 1.

Rep rows 2 and 3 until there are 25 sts.

Purl next row.

Row 25: With B, skp, knit across, k2tog.

Row 26: With B, purl.

Rep rows 25 and 26 until there are 3 sts remaining. Sk2p, cut string. Bind off last stitch.

Placement Diagram

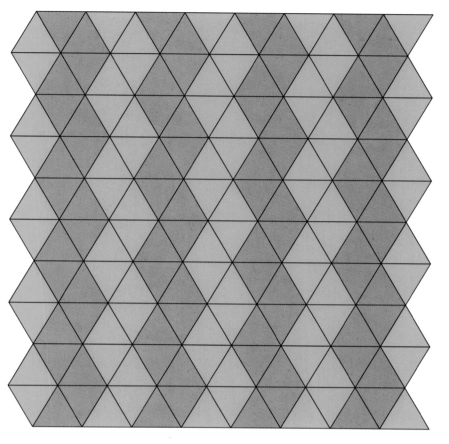

 parallelogram

Afghan

Make 80 parallelograms. Seam the parallelograms according to placement diagram.

Finishing

Weave the ends in.

Fringe

Make 160 (80 each in A and B. The general instructions for making fringe are on page 20. Make fringes by wrapping the yarn four times around the width of the cardboard strip. Attach 10 fringes to each corresponding color on the edge of the afghan. Repeat for other edge.

This afghan was knit with:

(A) 2 one-pound cones of Muench Yarns' *Cleo*, 87% viscose/ 13% metal yarn, medium, worsted weight, approx 564yd/515m per cone, color #135

(B) 2 one-pound cones of Muench Yarns' *Cleo*, 87% viscose/ 13% metal yarn, medium, worsted weight, approx. 564yd/515m per cone, color #121

mosaic masterpiece

With its repetitive design and intriguing color changes, this afghan seems complicated, like the intricate mosaic tile work that inspired it. Truth is, it's surprisingly easy to make. Handpainted and gossamer yarns create a variety of shades accented with flashes of shiny gold.

Finished Measurements

37 x 48"/95 x 122cm, blocked

Yarn

Approx total: 1408yd/1287m mohair/wool blend, medium weight yarn

Color A: 792yd/724m of red

Color B: 616yd/563m of white

Color C: Approx total: 666yd/609m mohair/nylon blend, medium weight yarn

Materials

Knitting needles: 6mm (Size 10 U.S.) *or size to obtain gauge*

Yarn bobbins

Tapestry needle for weaving the ends

Large crochet hook for attaching the fringe

Cardboard strip, 5"/12.7cm wide, for making the fringe

Gauge

16 sts = 4"/10cm over St st using Color A or B.
Always take time to check your gauge.

Pattern Note

For Color BC, hold one strand each of B and C together. The border stitches are worked in A.

Special Abbreviations

Sl wyif: Slip with the yarn in front.

Sl wyib: Slip with the yarn in back.

Pattern Stitch

MOSAIC MASTERPIECE STITCH (CHART A)

Row 1 (RS): With BC, k1, *k7, [sl 1, k1] 3 times, sl 1; rep from *, end k1.

Row 2 and all WS rows: P the purl sts, sl wyif all sl sts.

Row 3: With A, k1, * sl 1, k7, [sl 1, k1] 3 times; rep from *, end k1.

Row 5: With BC, k2, * sl 1, k7, [sl 1, k1] 3 times; rep from * to end.

Row 7: With A, *[k1, sl 1] twice, k7, sl 1, k1, sl 1; rep from *, end k2.

Row 9: With BC, k2, * sl 1, k1, sl 1, k7, [sl 1, k1] twice; rep from * to end.

Row 11: With A, *[k1, sl 1] 3 times, k7, sl 1; rep from *, end k2.

Row 13: With BC, k1, *[k1, sl 1] 3 times, k7, sl 1; rep from *, end k1.

Row 15: With A, k1, *[sl 1, k1] 3 times, sl 1, k7; rep from *, end k1.

Row 17: With BC, rep row 1.

Row 19: With A, *k7, [sl 1, k1] 3 times, sl 1; rep from *, end k2.

Row 21: With BC, k6, * [sl 1, k1] 3 times, sl 1, k7; rep from *, end last repeat k3.

Row 23: With A, k5, * [sl 1, k1] 3 times, sl 1, k7; rep from *, end last repeat k4.

Row 25: With BC, k4, * [sl 1, k1] 3 times, sl 1, k7; rep from *, end last repeat k5.

Row 27: With A, k3, * [sl 1, k1] 3 times, sl 1, k7; rep from *, end last repeat k6.

Row 29: With BC, k2, * [sl 1, k1] 3 times, sl 1, k7; rep from * to end.

Row 31: With A, rep row 15.

Row 32: Work row 2.

Rep rows 1–32 for pat.

Afghan

With A, CO 140 stitches. Work four rows in the garter stitch. Keeping four border stitches at the beginning and end of each row in the garter stitch in A, work from the pattern until the afghan measures 47½"/120.7cm. With A, work four rows in the garter stitch. Bind off all sts.

Finishing

Weave the ends in. Block according to the manufacturer's directions.

Fringe

Make enough to attach across the two edges of the afghan. The general instructions for making fringe are on page 20. Using A, wrap the yarn six times around the width of the cardboard strip. Attach to the edges and trim the ends of the fringe.

Design Tip

In order to keep the afghan flat during blocking, place heavy books on the corners after pinning.

Chart A

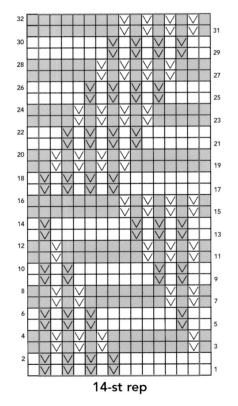

14-st rep

(white)	With color BC: K on RS, P on WS
V (white)	With color BC: Sl 1 wyib on RS; Sl 1 wyif on WS
(gray)	With color A: K on RS, P on WS
V (gray)	With color A: Sl 1 wyib on RS; Sl 1 wyif on WS

This afghan was knit with:

(A) 9 hanks of Brown Sheep Company's *Handpaint Originals*, 70% mohair/ 30% wool yarn, medium, worsted weight, 1.75oz/50g = approx 88yd/80m per hank, color #HP40 Strawberry Patch

(B) 7 hanks of Brown Sheep Company's *Handpaint Originals*, 70% mohair/ 30% wool yarn, medium, worsted weight, 1.75oz/50g = approx 88yd/80m per hank, color #HP85 Cream Puff

(C) 3 hanks of Karabella Yarns' *Gossamer*, 30% Kid mohair/ 52%nylon/18%polyester, medium, worsted weight 1.5oz/50g = 222yd/203m per hank, color #6300

wintry nights

Let winter come—this mohair-blend afghan, made with triple strands of yarn that are knit together, will keep you warm no matter how low the temperature falls. It's so easy to knit and quick to complete, it makes a perfect gift for any occasion.

Finished Measurements

35 x 53"/89 x 135cm, blocked

Yarn

Approx total: 3627yd/3317m mohair/wool/nylon blend, medium weight yarn

Color A: 651yd/595m in dark green

Color B: 651yd/595m in dark brown

Color C: 651yd/595m in light brown

Color D: 558yd/510m in tan

Color E: 558yd/510m in gray

Color F: 558yd/510m in lavender/gray blend

Materials

Knitting needles: 6.0mm (Size 10 U.S.) *or size to obtain gauge*

Tapestry hook for weaving the ends

Large crochet hook for attaching the tassels

Cardboard strip, 5"/12.7cm wide, for making the tassels

Gauge

12 sts and 16 rows = 4"/10cm over St st using G or H (see pattern note)
Always take time to check your gauge.

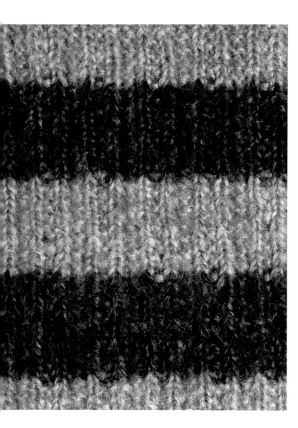

Pattern Note

For Color G, hold one strand each of A, B, and C together throughout. For Color H, hold one strand each of D, E, and F together throughout. There are seven pattern sections of H and eight pattern sections of G.

Special Abbreviations

K3 tbl: Knit three stitches through the back loop

Design Tip

Make sure that your tension is loose since each strand of yarn is very thin. For easier knitting, you can wind up the three yarns that will be knit together into one ball.

Pattern Stitch

WINTRY NIGHTS STITCH (CHART A)

Row 1 (RS): *P1, k1; repeat from* to last st, p1.

Row 2: K3 tbl, *p3, k3 tbl; repeat from* to end.

Rep rows 1 and 2 for Wintry Nights pat.

Afghan

With A, CO 123 sts. *With G, work the pattern for 14 rows (one pattern section). Change to H, work the pattern for 14 rows. Rep from* until seven sections of H and eight sections of G are completed. Bind off all stitches.

Tassel

Make 21 tassels in G, and 20 in H. The general instructions for making tassels are on page 20. Wrap the yarn six times around the width of the cardboard strip. Alternate 11 G and 10 H along one edge of the afghan beginning with G and ending with G. Attach the tassels 2"/5cm apart, then repeat for other side. Trim the ends of the tassels.

Finishing

Weave the ends in. Block lightly.

Chart A

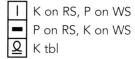

6-st rep

I	K on RS, P on WS
—	P on RS, K on WS
Ω	K tbl

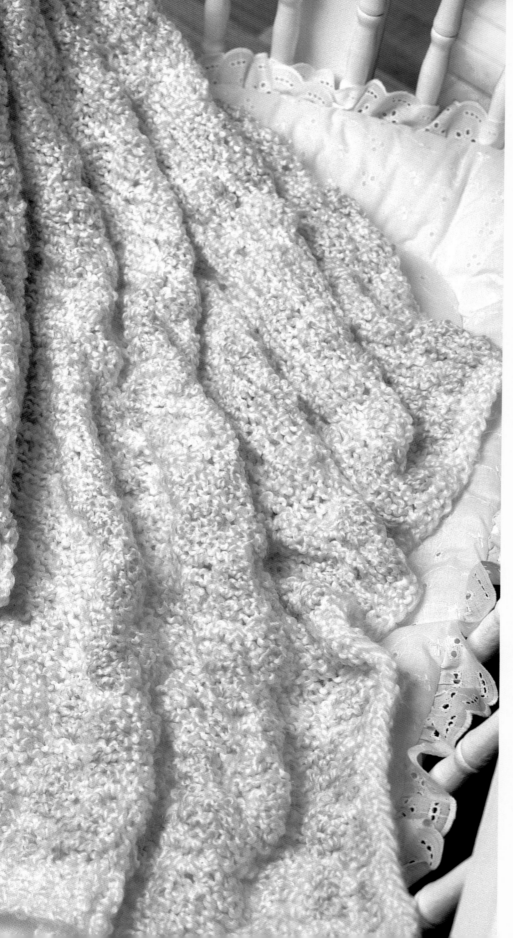

little
toes

Excitement over the arrival of
the newest member of
the family is so high that
baby projects seem to knit
themselves! This delicately
hued baby blanket is a lovely
project for beginning knitters
of all ages—it's easy to knit
and the yarn is smooth to
the touch. The drop stitch
makes soft puffs of yarn to
accommodate little toes.

SKILL LEVEL
Easy

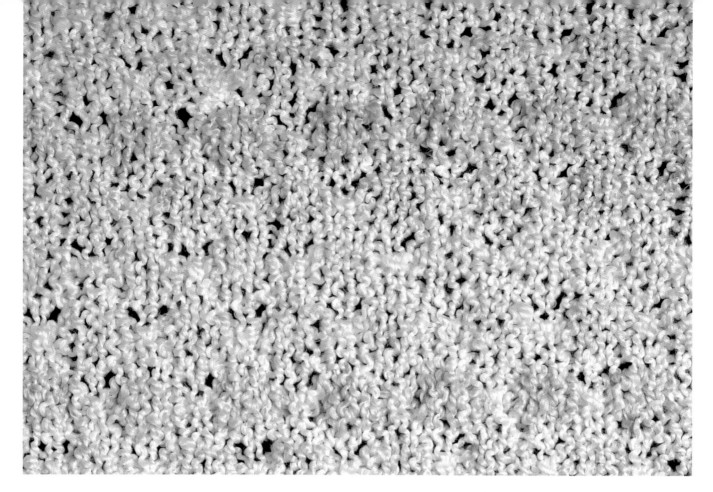

Finished Measurements

35 x38"/89 x 97cm

Yarn

Approx total: 744 yd/680m acrylic/ polyester blend, bulky weight yarn

Color A: 372yd/340m in white

Color B: 93yd/85m in violet

Color C: 93yd/85m in green

Color D: 93yd/85m in pink

Color E: 93yd/85m in blue

Materials

Knitting needles: 8mm (Size 11 U.S.) *or size to obtain gauge*

Yarn bobbins

Tapestry needle for weaving the ends

Gauge

12 sts and 16 rows = 4"/10cm over St st.

Always take time to check your gauge.

Pattern Note

The border stitches are worked in A.

Special Abbreviations

Drop st 4 rows down (D4): Drop the next stitch and let it unravel down four rows. Insert RH needle into the fifth row (Color A) from front to back and knit, catching all of the four loose strands.

Design Tip

This afghan is great for using leftover yarns since the four rows of the color pattern use small amounts of yarn.

Pattern Stitch

LITTLE TOES STITCH (CHART A)

Rows 1 and 3 (RS): With B, knit.

Rows 2 and 4: With B, purl.

Row 5: With A, K3, *D4, k3; rep from *.

Row 6: With A, purl.

Rows 7, 8, 9, and 10: With C, rep rows 1, 2, 3, and 4.

Row 11: With A, K1, *D4, k3; repeat from *, end last repeat with k1 instead of k3.

Row 12: With A, purl.

Rows 13, 14, 15, and 16: With D, repeat rows 1, 2, 3, and 4.

Rows 17 and 18: With A, repeat rows 5 and 6.

Rows 19, 20, 21, and 22: With E, repeat rows 1, 2, 3, and 4.

Rows 23 and 24: With A, repeat rows 11 and 12.

Rep rows 1–24 for pat.

Afghan

With A, CO 75 stitches. Knit two rows and purl the next row. Keeping four stitches at the beginning and end of each row in the garter stitch in A, work rows 1–24 six times, then repeat rows 1–6 once more from the pattern. With A, work two rows in the garter stitch. Bind off all stitches.

Finishing

Weave the ends in.

Chart A

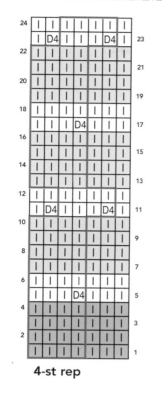

4-st rep

| I | K on RS, P on WS |
| D4 | Drop st 4 rows down |

This afghan was knit with:

(A) 4 skeins of Lion Brand Yarn's *Homespun Baby*, 98% acrylic/ 2% polyester yarn, bulky, chunky weight, 3oz/85g = approx 93yd/85m per skein, color #100 Snow White

(B) 1 skein of Lion Brand Yarn's *Homespun Baby*, 98% acrylic/ 2% polyester yarn, bulky, chunky weight, 3oz/85g = approx 93yd/85m per skein, color #144 Soft Violet

(C) 1 skein of Lion Brand Yarn's *Homespun Baby*, 98% acrylic/ 2% polyester yarn, bulky, chunky weight, 3oz/85g = approx 93yd/85m per skein, color #169 Soft Lime

(D) 1 skein of Lion Brand Yarn's *Homespun Baby*, 98% acrylic/ 2% polyester yarn, bulky, chunky weight, 3oz/85g = approx 93yd/85m per skein, color #101 Carnation

(E) 1 skein of Lion Brand Yarn's *Homespun Baby*, 98% acrylic/ 2% polyester yarn, bulky, chunky weight, 3oz/85g = approx 93 yd/ 85m per skein, color #105 Powder blue

sporting plaid

Go team! Made with three colors of soft chunky yarn, and knitted in the stockinette stitch, this afghan is a simplified version of the classic plaid blankets that sports fans love. The pattern graph makes it an ideal project for beginners who'd like to try their hand with multiple colors.

Finished Measurements

40 x 60"/102 x 152cm

Yarn

Approx total: 1320yd/1207m acrylic/nylon blend chunky weight yarn

Color A: 480yd/439m in black

Color B: 240yd/220m in white

Color C: 600yd/549m in multi-black/white

Materials

Knitting needles: 6mm (Size 10 U.S.) *or size to obtain gauge*

Yarn bobbins

Tapestry needle for weaving the ends

Large crochet hook for attaching the fringe

Cardboard strip, 5"/12.7cm wide, for making the fringe

Gauge

14 sts and 20 rows = 4"/10cm over St st
Always take time to check your gauge.

Pattern Note

When changing colors, pick up the new color under the old to avoid making holes (see *Intarsia* on page 16). For easier handling of several colors, make yarn bobbins. The chart does not show the border and edge stitches. The entire color chart pattern is worked in the stockinette stitch. Twenty-eight rows make up each plaid rectangle.

Afghan

With A, CO 144 stitches. Work four rows in the garter stitch in A. Keep four stitches in the garter stitch in A at the beginning and end of each row throughout. Work from the chart in the color pattern using the stockinette stitch. Once the color pattern is complete, work four rows in the garter stitch in A. Bind off all sts.

Finishing

Weave the ends in.

Fringe

Make enough fringes to attach across the two edges of the afghan. The general instructions for making fringe are on page 20. Using A, wrap the yarn six times around the width of the cardboard strip. Repeat using C. Attach A and C alternately to the edges and trim the ends of the fringe.

Design Tip

To keep the white yarn clean, place it in a plastic bag when knitting"

Chart A

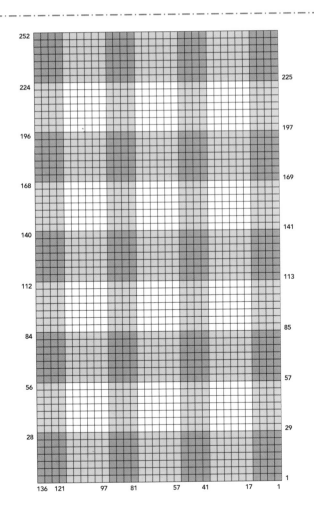

This afghan was knit with:

(A) 4 skeins of Stylecraft Yarns' *Charleston*, 67% acrylic/33% nylon yarn, bulky, chunky weight, 100g = approx 120yd/110m per skein, color # 5191 Chaplin

(B) 2 skeins of Stylecraft Yarns' *Charleston*, 67% acrylic/33% nylon yarn, bulky, chunky weight, 100g = approx 120yd/110m per skein, color # 5192 Garbo

(C) 5 skeins of Stylecraft Yarns' *Charleston*, 67% acrylic/33% nylon yarn, bulky, chunky weight, 100g = approx 120yd/110m per skein, color # 5190 Valentino

mocha café

You don't have to knit this ribbon afghan at your favorite coffee house, but its three colors—looking like latté, cappuccino, and espresso—make it tempting to do so. The afghan is made by knitting 36 blocks that you attach to one another—the result is a unique design reminiscent of Celtic spirals. This project will give intermediate knitters a good challenge.

Finished Measurements

Afghan: 45 x 48"/114 x 122cm, blocked

Squares: 7 x 8"/18 x 20cm

Yarn

Approx total: 1200yd/1097m rayon, medium weight yarn

Color A: 600yd/549m in white

Color B: 600yd/549m in light brown

Color C: Approx total: 600yd/549m merino wool/acetate blend, bulky weight yarn

Materials

Knitting needles: 5.5mm (Size 9 U.S.) *or size to obtain gauge*

Yarn bobbins

Tapestry needle for sewing the seams and weaving the ends

Size H-8/5mm crochet hook for making the edging and attaching the tassels

Cardboard strip, 5½"/14cm wide, for making the tassels

Gauge

18 sts and 20 rows = 4"/10cm over St st using strand of A or B.

16 sts and 20 rows = 4"/10cm over St st using strand of C.

Always take time to check your gauge.

Pattern Note

There are six rows of six squares each for a total of 36 squares in the afghan.

Squares

With C, CO 30 sts. Begin working from the color chart, beginning with row 1. Bind off all the stitches after completing row 43 of chart. Make 36 squares.

Design Tip

Knitting more dark brown stitches in place of the light brown stitches will make the swirl appear larger.

Chart A

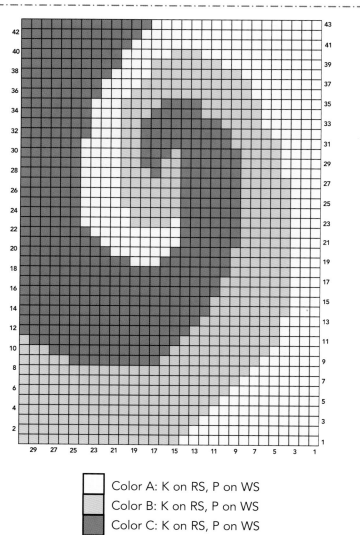

Color A: K on RS, P on WS
Color B: K on RS, P on WS
Color C: K on RS, P on WS

Afghan

With A, seam the squares together according to the placement diagram using the mattress stitch. The general instructions for the mattress stitch are on page 19.

Finishing

Weave the ends in and block.

Placement Chart

Square

Crochet Edging

Rnd 1: Using A, with the crochet hook facing RS, work one round of single crochet evenly around the outside edge of afghan.

Rnd 2: Slip stitch in the first stitch, chain three, double crochet in the next stitch, and then double crochet evenly around.

Rnd 3: With B, slip stitch in the first stitch, chain three, chain one, and then single crochet evenly around.

Tassels

Make four. The general instructions for making tassels are on page 20. Using C, wrap the yarn seven times around the width of the cardboard strip. Trim the edges of each tassel. Attach the tassels to all four corners of the afghan.

This afghan was knit with:

(A) 8 hanks of Berroco Yarns' *Glace*, 100% rayon, medium, worsted yarn, 1.75oz/50g = approx 75yd/69m per hank, color #2657

(B) 8 hanks of Berroco Yarns' *Glace*, 100% rayon, medium, worsted yarn, 1.75oz/50g = approx 75yd/69m per hank, color #2003

(C) 10 hanks of Berroco Yarns' *Chai*, 60% merino wool/40% acetate, bulky, chunky yarn, 1.75oz/50g = approx 60yd/55m per hank, color #9317

sleek and soft

This afghan begins with a shiny ribbed panel that blends into a soft mohair center. The pattern is suitable for beginners, and will deliver stunning results.

Finished Measurements

40 x 51"/102 x 130cm

Yarn

Color A: Approx total: 855yd/782m rayon/nylon blend, lightweight yarn

Color B: Approx total: 540yd/494m of mohair/acrylic/viscose/nylon/metal blend, bulky weight yarn

Materials

Knitting needles: 5mm (Size 8 U.S.) *or size to obtain gauge*

Tapestry needle for weaving the ends

Large crochet hook for attaching the fringe

Cardboard strip, 5"/12.7cm wide, for making the fringe

Gauge

20 sts = 4"/10cm over St st using A

16 sts = 4"/10cm over St st using B

Always take time to check your gauge.

Pattern Note

The center of the afghan will be worked in the stockinette stitch in Color B and the rib section in Color A. This afghan will have a slight hourglass shape.

This afghan was knit with:

(A) 9 balls of Trendsetter Yarns' *Sunshine,* 75% rayon/25% nylon yarn, DK, light worsted weight, 1.75oz/50g = approx 95yd/85m per ball, color #39

(B) 6 balls of Trendsetter Yarns' *Dune,* 41% Mohair/30% Acrylic/ 12% Viscose/11% Nylon/ 6% Metal, bulky, chunky weight 1.75oz/50g = approx 90yd/82m per ball, color #68

Pattern Stitch

RIB STITCH

Row 1 (RS): With A, *K8, p8, rep from *, end with k8.

Row 2: *P8, k8, rep from *, end with p8.

Rep rows 1–2 for rib pat.

Afghan

With A, CO 168 sts. Work in the rib pat for 17"/43.2cm. Change to B, work in the stockinette stitch for 17"/43.2cm. Change to A, work the rib pat for 17"/43.2cm. Bind off.

Finishing

Weave the ends in.

Fringe

You will make 60 fringes using A and 36 fringes using B. The general instructions for making fringe are on page 20. Wrap the yarn seven times around the width of the cardboard strip. Attach to the edges by placing three A fringes on the knit stitches and two B fringes on purl stitches, repeat to the end, ending with three fringes in A. Trim the ends of the fringe.

Design Tip

Since the metallic yarn has a fine texture, it can easily catch on rough nails or jewelry. Filing your nails and removing any jewelry before working will minimize this.

mother's moment

This afghan, designed by our mother, offers a simple design with spectactular results. Each block is knitted separately using the bramble stitch. The easy cable border is a perfect complement to the afghan's lush texture.

SKILL LEVEL
Easy

Finished Measurements

50 x 60"/127 x 152cm, blocked, with cable border

Yarn

Approx total: 2470yd/2258m wool/mohair blend, medium weight yarn

Color A: 1330yd/1216m in blue

Color B: 1140yd/1042m in light blue

Materials

Knitting needles: 6mm (Size 10 U.S.) *or size to obtain gauge*

Cable needle

Tapestry needle for sewing the seams and attaching the cable border

Crochet hook for attaching the tassels

Cardboard strip, 6"/15.2cm wide, for making the tassels

Gauge

22 sts and 20 rows = 4"/10cm over Bramble Stitch

Always take time to check your gauge.

Pattern Note

There are 12 rows of 10 squares each for a total of 120 squares in the afghan Cable borders are worked separately, then sewn to the edges.

Special Abbreviations

10-st right cable: Slip 5 stitches to the cable needle and hold to back of work, k5, k5 from cable needle.

Pattern Stitch

BRAMBLE STITCH

Row 1 (RS): Purl.

Row 2 (WS): K1, *(k1, p1, k1) into next stitch, p3tog; repeat from * to last stitch, end with k1.

Row 3: Purl.

Row 4: K1, *p3tog, (k1, p1, k1) into next stitch; repeat from * to last stitch, end with k1.

Rep rows 1–4 for pat.

Squares

Make 60 in A and 60 in B. CO 22 sts and work in pat for 20 rows. Bind off.

Joining Squares

With A or B, seam squares together according to the placement diagram.

Cable Border (Chart A)

Make four borders in A.

CO 16 sts.

Rows 1 and 3 (RS): P3, k10, p3.

Rows 2 and all WS: K3, p10, k3.

Row 5: P3, 10-st right cable, p3.

Row 7: Rep row 1.

Row 8: Rep row 2.

Rep rows 1–8 for the cable border pat.

Knit two of the cable borders until they each measure 46"/117cm, then knit the other two until each is 60"/152.4cm. Bind off.

Cable Border (Chart A)

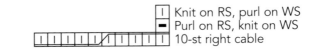

I Knit on RS, purl on WS
- Purl on RS, knit on WS
10-st right cable

Placement Chart

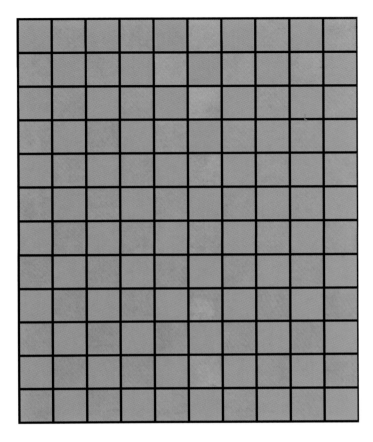

Joining Cable Borders to Afghan

Attach the 60"/152cm cable borders to the two long edges of the afghan, then attach the 46"/117cm cables to the top and bottom edges, which now include the top and bottom edges of the longer attached cable borders.

Finishing

Block the afghan after attaching the cable borders. Be careful not to flatten the knit.

Tassels

Make four. The general instructions for making tassels are on page 20. Using A, wrap the yarn 24 times around the width of the cardboard strip, then wrap B around the head, leaving a length of yarn for attachment. Trim the edges of each tassel. Attach the tassels to all four corners of the afghan.

Design Tip

This is an easy afghan for those who want to create an heirloom that will last for generations.

This afghan was knit with:

(A) 7 skeins of Brown Sheep Company's *Lamb's Pride Worsted*, 85% wool/15% mohair, medium, worsted weight, 4oz/113g = approx 190yd/174m per skein, color #M77 Blue Magic

(B) 6 skeins of Brown Sheep Company's *Lamb's Pride Worsted*, 85% wool/15% mohair, medium, worsted weight, 4oz/112g = approx 190yd/174m per skein, color #M76 Misty Blue

the highlands

Raised bands of gold velvet enhance the shimmering green base. For variation, keep the gold bands and use any other color of your choice. The result will be equally wonderful—a super-elegant afghan that is easy to knit and a welcome gift to receive.

Finished Measurements

50 x 55"/127 x 140cm

Yarn

Approx total: 1202yd/1100m viscose, bulky weight yarn

Color A: 656yd/600m in green

Color B: 546yd/500m in gold

Materials

Knitting needles: 6.5mm (Size 10 U.S.) *or size to obtain gauge*

Tapestry needle for weaving the ends

Yarn bobbins

Large crochet hook for attaching the fringe

Cardboard strip, 3"/7.6cm wide, for making the fringe

Gauge

11 sts and 16 rows = 4"/10cm over St st .
Always take time to check your gauge.

Pattern Note

The border stitches and rows 4 and 5 are worked with color B only.

Special Abbreviations

Inc 1: Knit in front then in back of the stitch.

Pattern Stitch

THE HIGHLANDS STITCH (CHART A)

Row 1 (WS): With A, purl.

Row 2 (RS): With A, knit.

Row 3: With A, purl.

Row 4: With B, knit into front and back of each st.

Row 5: With B, *k2tog; rep from * to end.

Row 6: With A, knit.

Row 7: With A, purl.

Row 8: With A, knit.

Repeat rows 1–8 for pat.

Design Tip

For changing the colors, use bobbins.

Afghan

With B, CO 114 sts. Work four rows in the garter stitch. Keeping four sts at the beginning and end of each row in the garter stitch in B, work rows 1–8 from the pattern until the afghan measures 54½"/138.4cm. Change to B, work four rows in the garter stitch. Bind off all stitches.

Finishing

Weave the ends in.

Fringe

Make enough fringes to attach across the two edges of the afghan. The general instructions for making fringe are on page 20. Using A, wrap the yarn four times around the width of the cardboard strip. Repeat using B. When attaching the fringes to the edges, *attach one fringe of A, and three fringes of B; repeat from * across, ending with A, then trim the ends of the fringe.

Chart A

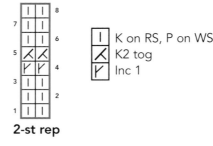

	K on RS, P on WS
	K2 tog
	Inc 1

2-st rep

This afghan was knit with:

(A) 6 hanks of Colinette Yarns' *Isis*, 100% viscose, super bulky, bulky weight, 100g = approx 109yd/100m per hank, color #113 Velvet Leaf

(B) 5 hanks of Colinette Yarns' *Isis*, 100% viscose, super bulky, bulky weight, 100g = approx 109yd/100m per hank, color #112 Velvet Gold

perfect pearls

Special occasions such as weddings, anniversaries, and births will be graced by the gift of this lustrous beaded afghan. Stringing the pearls on the yarn before beginning to knit is the key to carefree, uninterrupted knitting.

SKILL LEVEL
Intermediate

Finished Measurements

40 x 50"/102 x 127cm, blocked

Yarn

Approx total: 1360yd/1244m acrylic, medium weight yarn

Materials

Knitting needles: 5.0mm (Size 8 U.S.) *or size to obtain gauge*

Six hundred 6mm white pearl beads

Tapestry needle for weaving the ends

Gauge

20 sts = 4"/10cm over St st
Always take time to check your gauge.

Pattern Note

String the yarn with the beads.

Special Abbreviations

Skp: Slip one stitch. Knit next stitch and pass the slip stitch over the knit stitch.

Sk2p with bead: Slip one stitch, knit two stitches together with the bead pushed forward. Pass the slipped stitch over the bead.

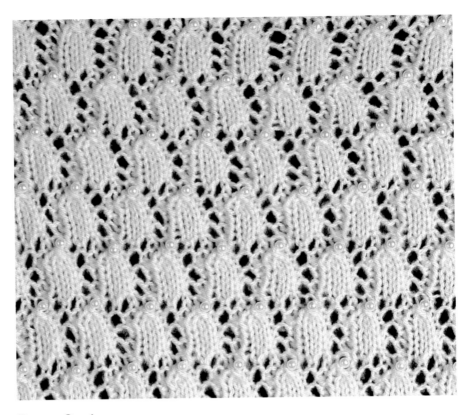

Pattern Stitch

PERFECT PEARLS STITCH (CHART A)

Rows 1, 3, 5, and 7(WS): P3, *k3, p3, rep from* to end.

Rows 2 and 6: K3, *p2tog, yo, p1, k3, rep from* to end.

Row 4: K3, *p1, yo, p2tog, k3, rep from* to end.

Row 8: K1, k2tog, *[p1, yo] twice, p1, sk2p with bead, rep from*, end last repeat skp, k1, instead of sk2p.

Rows 9, 11, 13, and 15: K3, *p3, k3, rep from* to end.

Rows 10 and 14: P1, yo, p2tog, *k3, p1, yo, p2tog, rep from* to end.

Row 12: P2tog, yo, p1, *k3, p2tog, yo, p1, rep from* to end.

Row 16: P2, yo, p1, *sk2p with bead, [p1, yo] twice, p1, rep from* to last 6 sts, sk2p with bead, p1, yo, p2.

Rep rows 1–16 for pat.

SEED STITCH

Row 1 (RS): *K1, p1; rep from* across.

Row 2: P the knit sts and k the purl sts

Rep row 2 for seed st.

Stringing the Yarn with beads

See page 16.

Design Tip

It's easier to string the beads on the yarn and knit with them rather than sew them on the afghan later.

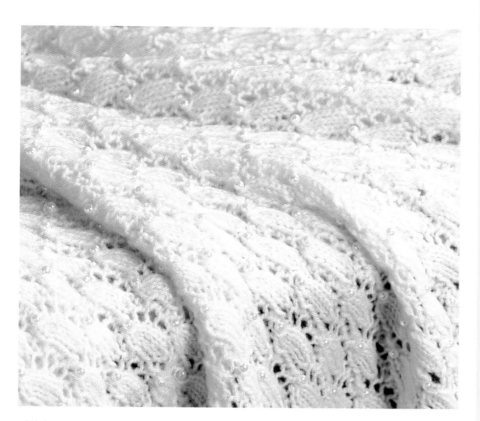

Afghan

CO 137 stitches. Work four rows in the seed stitch. Keeping four stitches at the beginning and the end of each row in the seed stitch, begin the pattern. Work until the afghan measures 49½"/126cm. Work four rows in the seed stitch. Bind off all stitches.

Finishing

Weave the ends in.

Chart A

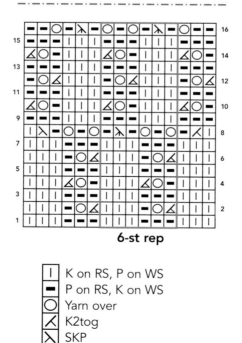

6-st rep

	K on RS, P on WS
	P on RS, K on WS
	Yarn over
	K2tog
	SKP
	Sk2p with bead
	P2tog

This afghan was knit with:

8 skeins of Reynolds Yarns' *Unger Fluffy*, 100% acrylic yarn, medium, worsted weight, 50g = approx 170yd/155m per skein, color #441

royal elegance

This luxurious afghan will feel right at home wrapped around your shoulders. Two different gold yarns—one velvety soft, the other thin and shiny—create a look that is both elegant and showy. The simple puffed bubble stitch gives this afghan its cozy thickness.

Finished Measurements

35 x 50"/ 89 x 127cm

Yarn

Color A: Approx total: 500yd/457m acrylic/rayon blend, bulky weight yarn

Color B: Approx total: 345yd/316m acrylic/cupro/polyester blend, medium weight yarn

Materials

Knitting needles: 8mm (Size 11 U.S.) *or size to obtain gauge*

Tapestry needle for weaving the ends

Large crochet needle for attaching the fringe

Cardboard strip, 5"/12.7cm wide, for making the fringe

Gauge

8 sts and 16 rows = 4"/10cm over St st using Color A

16 sts and 20 rows = 4"/10cm over St st using Color B

Always take time to check your gauge.

Pattern Note

Rows 4 and 5 are the only rows worked in Color B. Purl very loosely on row 5 so it will be easy to work row 6.

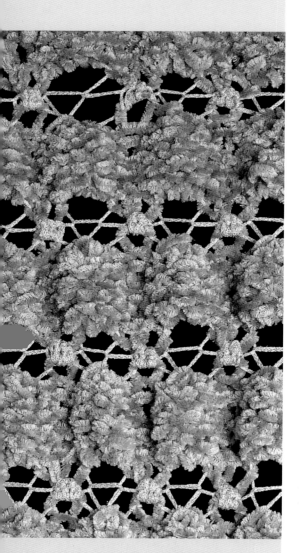

Pattern Stitch

ROYAL ELEGANCE STITCH (CHART A)

Row 1 (RS): With A, purl.

Row 2: With A, knit.

Row 3: With A, purl.

Row 4: With B, K1, p3tog, [k1, p1, k1, p1, k1] into next st, *p5tog, [k1, p1, k1, p1, k1] into next st; rep from * to last 4 sts, p3tog, k1.

Row 5: With B, purl loosely.

Row 6: With A, K1, [k1, p1, k1] into next st, p5tog, *[k1, p1, k1, p1, k1] into next st, p5tog; rep from * to last 2 sts, [k1, p1, k1] into next st, k1.

Row 7: With A, purl.

Row 8: With A, knit.

Rep rows 1–8 for pat.

Afghan

With A, CO 99 stitches. Begin working the pattern until the afghan measures 50"/127cm. Bind off all the stitches.

Finishing

Weave the ends in.

Fringe

The general instructions for making fringe are on page 20. Using B, wrap the yarn seven times around the width of the cardboard strip. Attach the fringe 2"/5cm apart along edges of afghan. Do not trim the bottom ends of the fringe.

Chart A

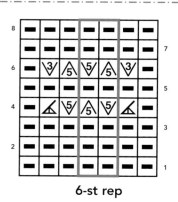

6-st rep

▬	P on RS, K on WS
⑤	Inc 5 by [k1,p1,k1,p1,k1] into next st
⑤	p5 tog
◺	P3tog
③	Inc 3 by [k1, p1, k1] into next st

Design Tip

In order to make it easier to change from a thinner thread to a thicker one, make sure to loosely work the row before the change.

This afghan was knit with:

(A) 5 skeins of Lion Brand Yarns' *Chenille Thick & Quick*, 91% acrylic/9% rayon yarn, super bulky, bulky weight, 5oz. = approx 100yd/91m per skein, color #124 Khaki

(B) 3 skeins of Lion Brand Yarns' *Glitterspun*, 60% acrylic/27% cupro/13% polyester yarn, medium, worsted weight, 1.75oz/50g = approx 115 yd/105m per skein, color #170 Gold

classic impressions

If you've been waiting for the right cable pattern, this is it! This handsome afghan is sure to impress all who see it, and will serve as a showcase for your knitting skills.

SKILL LEVEL
Intermediate

Finished Measurements

36 x 47"/91 x 119cm, blocked

Yarn

Approx total: 1190 yd/1088m cotton/rayon, medium weight yarn

Materials

Knitting needles: 5.5mm (Size 9 U.S.) *or size to obtain gauge*

Tapestry needle for weaving the ends

Large crochet hook for attaching the fringe

Cardboard strip, 5½"/14cm wide, for making the fringe

Gauge

18 sts and 20 rows = 4"/10cm over St st

Always take time to check your gauge.

Special Abbreviations

2-st right twist [RT]: K2tog, leaving both sts on needle; insert RH needle between 2 sts, and k first st again; then sl both sts from needle.

4-st right purl cable: Sl 1 st to cn and hold to back of work, k3, p1 from cn.

4-st left purl cable: Sl 3 sts to cn and hold to front of work, p1, k3 from cn.

8-st left cable: Sl 4 sts to cn and hold to front of work, k4, k4 from cn.

Pattern Stitch

CLASSIC IMPRESSIONS CABLE STITCH (CHART A)

Row 1 (RS): P1, *4-st left purl cable, p8, 4-st right purl cable, p2; rep from* end last 17 sts, 4-st left purl cable, p8, 4-st right purl cable, p1.

Row 2 and all WS rows: K the knit sts, p the purl sts.

Row 3: P2, *4-st left purl cable, p6, 4-st right purl cable, p4; rep from * end last 16 sts, 4-st left purl cable, p6, 4-st right purl cable, p2.

Row 5: P3, *4-st left purl cable, p4, 4-st right purl cable, p6; rep from* end last 15 sts, 4-st left purl cable, p4, 4-st right purl cable, p3.

Row 7: P4, *4-st left purl cable, p2, 4-st right purl cable, p3, RT, p3; rep from* end last 14 sts, 4-st left purl cable, p2, 4-st right purl cable, p4.

Row 9: P5, *8-st left cable, p4, RT, p4; rep from* end last 13 sts, 8-st left cable, p5.

Row 11: P5, *k8, p4, RT, p4; rep from* end last 13 sts, k8, p5.

Row 13: Rep row 9.

Rows 15, 17, and 19: P5, *k3, p2, k3, p4, RT, p4, rep from* end last 13 sts, k3, p2, k3, p5.

Row 21: P4, *4-st right purl cable, p2, 4-st left purl cable, p8; rep from*; end last repeat p4 instead of p8.

Row 23: P3, *4-st right purl cable, p4, 4-st left purl cable, p6; rep from*; end last repeat p3 instead of p6.

Row 25: P2, *4-st right purl cable, p6, 4-st left purl cable, p4; rep from*; end last repeat p2 instead of p4.

Row 27: P1, *4-st right purl cable, p3, RT, p3, 4-st left purl cable, p2; rep from*; end last repeat p1 instead of p2.

Chart A

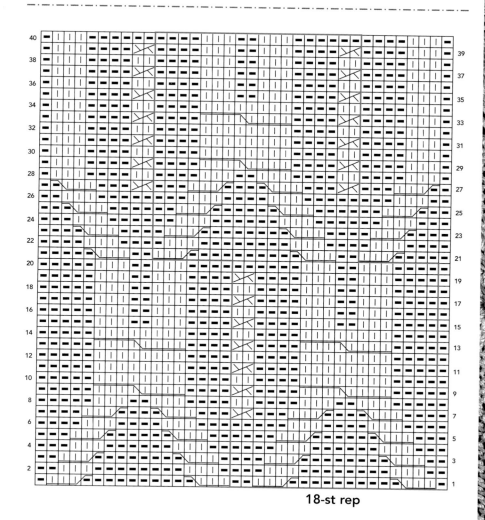

18-st rep

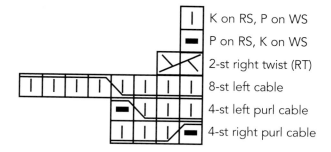

	K on RS, P on WS
	P on RS, K on WS
	2-st right twist (RT)
	8-st left cable
	4-st left purl cable
	4-st right purl cable

This afghan was knit with:

(A) 14 hanks of Berroco Yarns' *Cotton Twist*, 70% mercerized cotton/30% rayon yarn, medium, worsted weight, 1.75oz/50g = approx 85yd/78m per hank, color #8322

Row 29: P1, k3, *p4, RT, p4, 8-st left cable; rep from * end last 10 sts, RT, p4, k3, p1.

Row 31: P1, k3, *p4, RT, p4, k8; rep from * end last 10 sts, RT, p4, k3, p1.

Row 33: Rep row 29.

Rows 35, 37, and 39: P1, *k3, p4, RT, p4, k3, p2; rep from *; end last repeat p1 instead of p2.

Row 40: Work row 2.

Rep rows 1–40 for pat.

Seed Stitch

Row 1 (RS): *K1, p1; rep from * across.

Row 2: P the knit sts and k the purl sts.

Rep row 2 for seed st.

Design Tip

Enlarging the chart when photo-copying will make it easier to read.

Afghan

CO 152 stitches. Work four rows in the seed stitch. Work in the pattern until the afghan measures 46½"/118cm, keeping four border stitches at the beginning and end of each row in the seed stitch throughout. Work four rows in the seed stitch. Bind off all stitches.

Finishing

Weave the ends in.

Fringe

The general instructions for making a knotted fringe are on page 20. For the fringes, wrap the yarn eight times around the width of the cardboard strip. Each end of the afghan has a two-level knotted fringe. The base, or first level, is made of 10 knotted fringes with the second level having nine knots.

modern reflections

Paisley, the brightly patterned fabric with abstract swirling shapes, was first used in woven Kashmir shawls. In the mid-18th century, these shawls were brought back to Britain and adopted enthusiastically by textile artists in Paisley, Scotland. This cheery contemporary version combines contrasting earth tones with brightly colored embroidery and small round mirrors. The result is an eye-catching art piece that energizes the decor of any room.

SKILL LEVEL
Easy

Finished Measurements

53 x 57"/135 x 145cm

Yarn

Approx total: 1868yd/1708m acrylic, medium weight yarn

Color A: 1188yd/1086m in bronze

Color B: 680yd/622m in dark green

Color C: small amounts in bright red

Color D: small amounts in bright orange

Color E: small amounts in bright yellow

Color F: small amounts in bright turquoise

Color G: small amounts in bright purple

Color H: small amounts in bright green

Color I: small amounts in black

Materials

Knitting needles: 6.0mm (Size 10 U.S.) *or size to obtain gauge*

Forty 1"/2.5cm round mirrors

Eighteen 2"/5cm round mirrors

Washable fabric glue for attaching the mirrors

Tapestry needle for embroidery, attaching the pieces, and sewing the seams

Large crochet hook for attaching the tassels

Cardboard strip, 5½"/14cm wide, for making the tassels

Gauge

15 sts and 18 rows = 4"/10cm over St st

Always take time to check your gauge.

Pattern Note

The border squares will be slightly pointed at the corners after seaming squares together. The following embroidery stitches are used for this afghan: chain stitch, shisha stitch, French knots, and the lazy daisy stitch. General instructions for them are found on pages 17 and 18. All templates, except #7, show that the paisley motifs are outlined with one row of an embroidered chain stitch in black. The templates are on pages 150-156. Glue the mirrors to the afghan before working the shisha stitch.

PATTERN NOTES FOR THE TEMPLATES

Template 1: Place template 1 in the middle of the template 2 paisley as indicated in the placement diagram. As shown in the photo on page 150, with I, use the chain stitch to outline the outer edges of the paisley and the inner eye. With D, use the chain stitch to fill in the outer sections of the paisley. With C, use the chain stitch to fill in the inner eye.

Template 2: Enlarge the template three times. Place the template as indicated on the placement diagram. This template is the center paisley in the afghan. With I, use the chain stitch to outline the paisley. Moving in toward the center, use the chain stitch to follow the outline first in C, then again D, and finally in F. With I, use the chain stitch to outline the inside of the paisley as indicated in the photo on page 151. With C, use the chain stitch to make the teardrop on the inner outline. With E, use the chain stitch to make the teardrop outside of the paisley, as shown in the photo on page 151.

Template 3: Place the template as indicated on the placement diagram. With I, use the chain stitch to outline the outer edge of the paisley and to fill in the inner eye. As indicated in the photo on page 152, use the main colors C, F, G, or H, to fill in the six sections of the paisley, starting with the tail section. Chain stitch the teardrop in D or E, and make the French knot in the main color, as shown in template 3 and the photo on page 152.

Template 4: Place the templates as indicated on the placement diagram. With I, use the chain stitch to outline the outer edge of the paisley. With D, use the chain stitch to follow the outline in toward the center. With C, use the chain stitch to fill in as shown in the photo on page 153.

Template 5: Place the template as indicated on the placement diagram. With I, use the chain stitch to outline the outer edge of the paisley. With C, then D, use the chain stitch to follow the outline in toward the center. With F, use the chain stitch to fill in the center. With E, use the Lazy Daisy stitch around the edge of the paisley, as shown in the photo on page 154.

Template 6: Place the template as indicated on the placement diagram. With H, use the chain stitch to make the leaves. With I, use the chain stitch to fill in the middle stem in the leaves, as shown in the photo on page 155.

Template 7: Place the stem and leaves as indicated on the placement diagram. With H, use the chain stitch to make the stem. With C, D, E, and F use the chain stitch to make the leaves, as shown in the photo on page 156.

Special Abbreviations

Inc 1: Knit in front then in back of stitch.

Sk2p: Slip one stitch, knit two stitches together. Pass the slipped stitch over two stitches knit together.

Pattern Stitch

SEED STITCH

Row 1 (RS): *K1, p1; rep from * across.

Row 2: P the knit sts and k the purl sts.

Rep row 2 for seed st.

BORDER

Triangle

Make 72 in B

Row 1 (RS): With B, CO 3 sts.

Row 2: Purl.

Row 3: Inc 1, k across, Inc 1.

Rep rows 2 and 3 until there are 23 sts.

Work next five rows in seed st.

Bind off.

Diamond

Make 18 in A

Row 1 (RS): With A, CO 3 sts.

Row 2: Purl.

Row 3: Inc 1, k across, Inc 1.

Rep rows 2 and 3 until there are 23 sts.

Purl next Row.

fig. 1

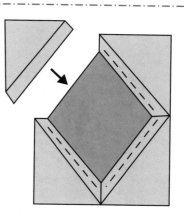

Row 25: Skp, knit across, k2tog.

Row 26: Purl.

Rep rows 25 and 26 until there are 3 sts remaining. Sk2p, cut string.

Center Panel

With A, CO 103 sts. K one row. Work in St st until afghan measures 34"/86cm. Bind off.

Asembling the Border

Note: The squares will become slightly elongated on the edges where the triangles connect, making them a diamond shape. Attach the four triangles to the diamond as shown in figure 1. Attach each of the triangles to the diamond first, then connect the triangles together at their common edges.

Design Tip

When embroidering the interior section of the afghan, using a large embroidery hoop will make the work easier to complete.

Placement Diagram

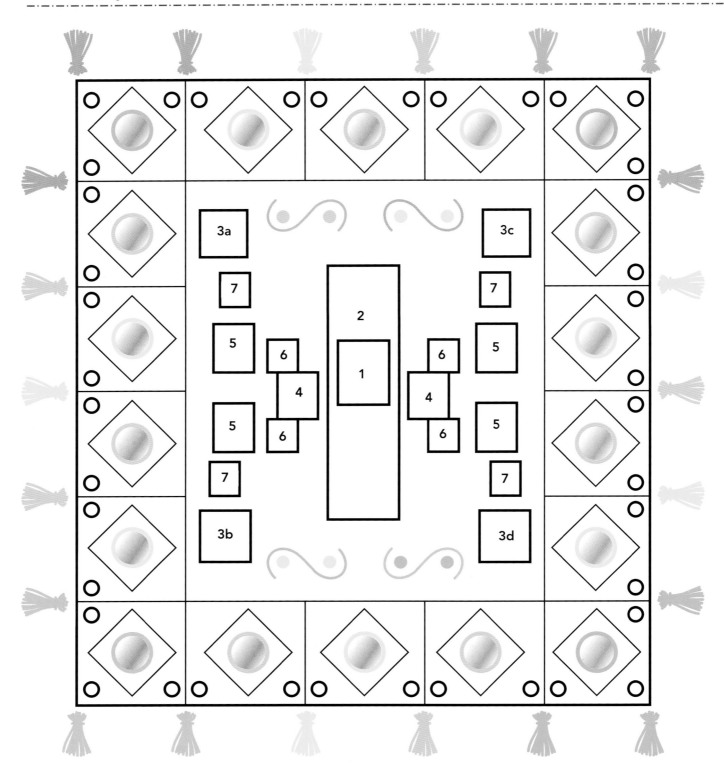

◯ Work shisha stitch on the large mirrors with the corresponding color.

● Work shisha stitch on the small mirror with black yarn.

1, 2, 3, 4, 5, 6, 7 Place corresponding template on the afghan and work embroidery sts according to the directions in Pattern Notes for the Templates on pages 146–147.

3a Work in the chain st; fill the six sections in alternating colors of purple and yellow. With purple, work the French knot as indicated on template 3. With yellow, work the chain-stitched teardrop as indicated on template 3.

3b Work in the chain st; fill the six sections in alternating colors of green and orange. With green, work the French knot as indicated on template 8. With orange, work the chain-stitched teardrop as indicated on template 3.

3c Work in the chain st; fill the six sections in alternating colors of blue and orange. With blue, work the French knot as indicated on template 3. With orange, work chain-stitch teardrops as indicated on template 3.

3d Work in the chain st; fill the six sections in alternating colors of red and yellow. With red, work the French knot as indicated on template 3. With yellow, work the chain-stitch teardrop as indicated on template 3.

◯ Work French knot either in orange or yellow.

〰 Work one row of chain st according to the shape and color.

 Place colored tassels according to diagram.

Joining the Border to the Center Panel

Follow the placement diagram to attach the border squares to the center panel using the mattress stitch. Using C, embroider one row of the chain stitch over the edge of the center panel to help it retain its shape.

Finishing

Weave the ends in and block. Referring to the general instructions for embroidery on pages 17 and 18, work the stitches according to the pattern note and templates on pages 150–157, position the embroidery as shown in the placement diagram.

Tassels

Make three each in C, F, G, and H and five in D and E. The general instructions for making tassels are on page 20. Wrap the yarn seven times around the width of the cardboard strip, then wrap the yarn to make the head, leaving a length of yarn for attachment. Trim the edges of each tassel. Attach the tassels according to the placement diagram.

Template 1

Use at 100%

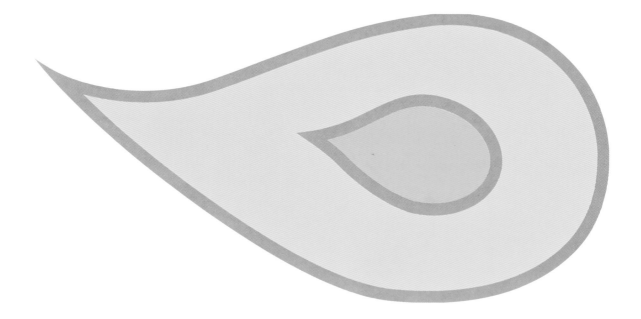

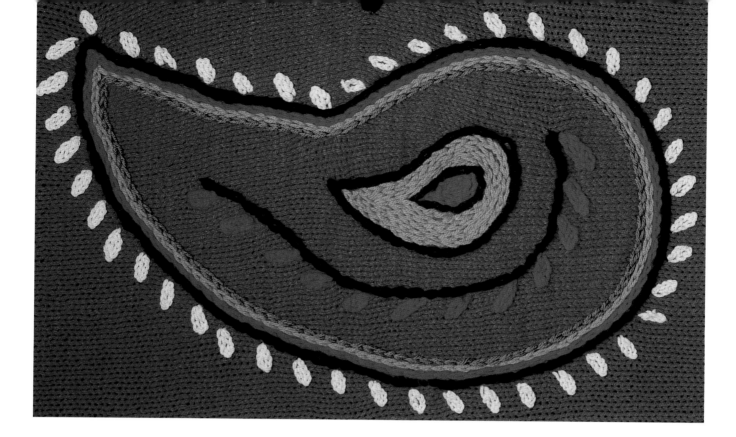

Template 2

Enlarge 270%

Template 3

Use at 100%

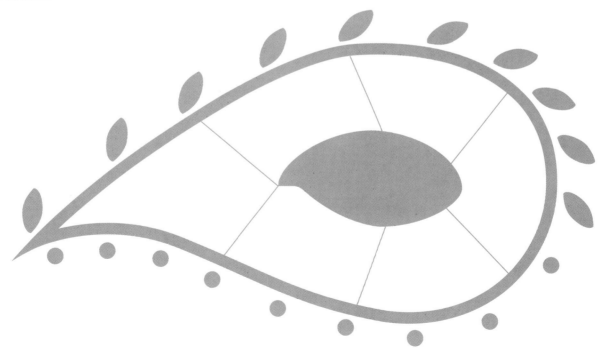

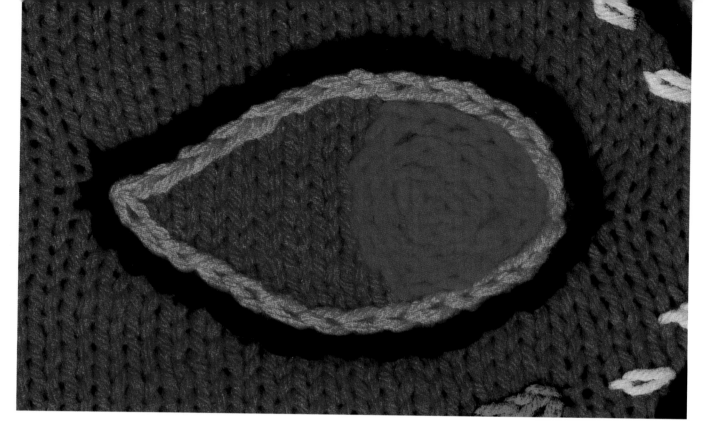

Template 4

Use at 100%

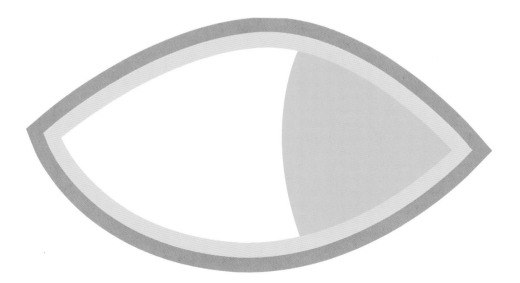

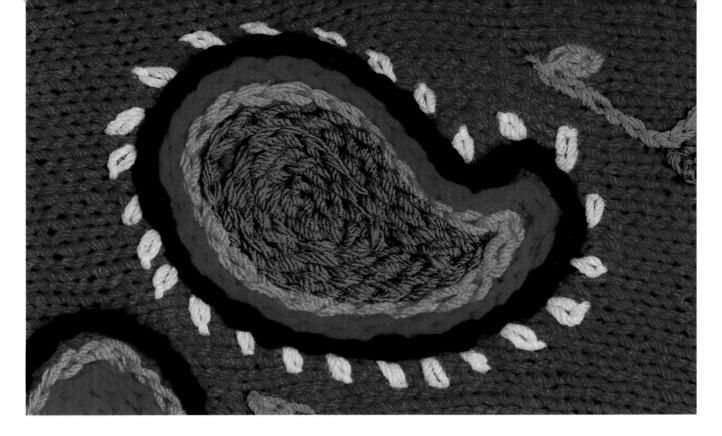

Template 5

Enlarge 140%

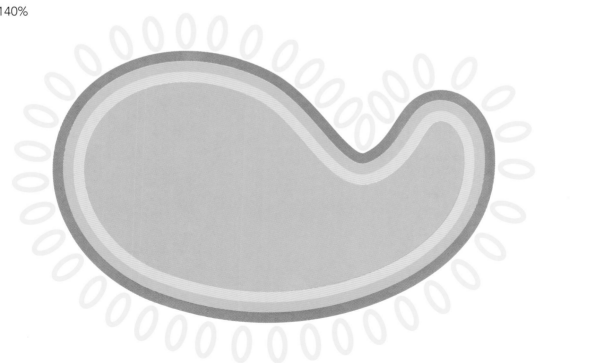

Template 6

Use at 100%

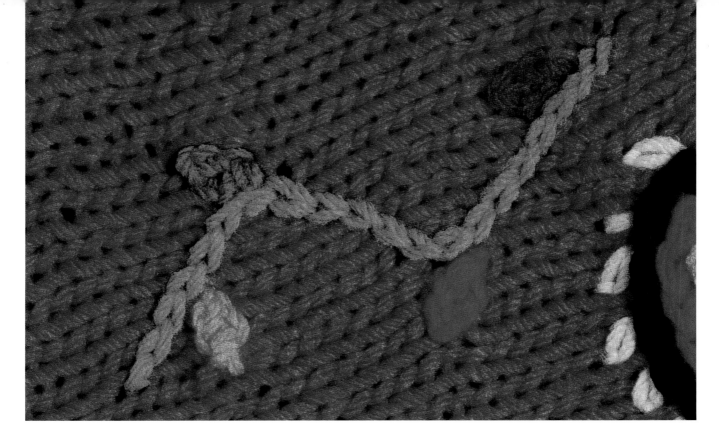

Template 7

Use at 100%

This afghan was knit with:

(A) 6 skeins of Coats & Clark Yarn's *Red Heart Classic,* 100% acrylic yarn, medium, worsted weight, 3.5oz/100g = approx 198yd/181m per skein, color #0286 Bronze

(B) 4 skeins of Coats & Clark Yarn's *Red Heart Super Saver,* 100% acrylic yarn, medium, worsted weight, 3oz/85g = approx 170yd/155m per skein, color #0391 Artichoke

(C) 1 skein of Coats & Clark Yarn's *Red Heart Classic,* 100% acrylic yarn, medium, worsted weight, 3.5oz/100g = approx 198yd/181m per skein, color #0912 Cherry Red

(D) 1 skein of Coats & Clark Yarn's *Red Heart Super Saver,* 100% acrylic yarn, medium, worsted weight, 3oz/85g = approx 170yd/155m per skein, color #0354 Vibrant Orange

(E) 1 skein of Coats & Clark Yarn's *Red Heart Super Saver,* 100% acrylic yarn, medium, worsted weight, 3oz/85g = approx 170yd/155m per skein, color #324 Bright Yellow

(F) 1 skein of Coats & Clark Yarn's *Red Heart Kids,* 100% acrylic yarn, medium, worsted weight, 5oz/141g = approx 302yd/276m per skein, color #2850 Turquoise

(G) 1 skein of Coats & Clark Yarn's *Red Heart Classic,* 100% acrylic yarn, medium, worsted weight, 3.5oz/100g = approx 198yd/181m per skein, color #0596 Purple

(H) 1 skein of Coats & Clark Yarn's *Red Heart Super Saver,* 100% acrylic yarn, medium, worsted weight, 3oz/85g = approx 170yd/155m per skein, color #0676 Emerald

(I) 1 skein of Coats & Clark Yarn's *Red Heart Classic,* 100% acrylic yarn, medium, worsted weight, 3.5oz/100g = approx 198yd/181m per skein, color #012 Black

The mirrors used were:

4 packages of Darice's *Mirrors* 1" Round Mirrors, 10pcs, item #1613-42

5 packages of Darice's *Mirrors* 2" Round Mirrors, 4pcs, item #1613-43

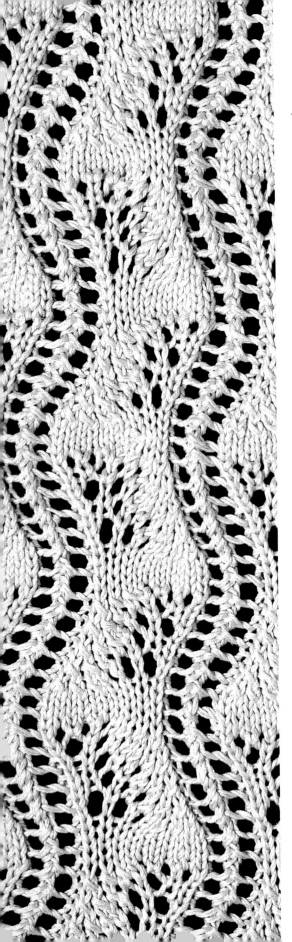

acknowledgments

We were privileged to have the support and assistance of a wide array of individuals play an integral part in the compilation and formation of this book. Our heartfelt tribute goes to those particular individuals whose continual encouragement cannot go unnoticed.

We were fortunate to have the opportunity to work with the staff at Lark Books. Everyone has been absolutely fantastic. Many thanks go to our editors, Marcianne Miller and Jane LaFerla, two wonderful sweet women. Jane, we could not have done this without you. Your patience and support in the last stages of our book has been vital in making this book a success. Special thanks from our hearts go to Marcianne Miller who has played a fundamental part in the outcome of our afghans. You have become a "mother hen" to us, guiding our progress patiently. Many thanks to Carol Taylor, who knew our potential before we knew it ourselves; to senior editor, Deborah Morganthal who made the transition a smooth ride; to Nicole Tuggle, you've been there from the beginning, thank you for your support; and to art director Stacey Budge, we have no words to express our gratitude for your sincere dedication in presenting our work. You are truly remarkable.

Many thanks go to the photographer, Stewart O'Shields. Your outstanding photographs were beyond our expectations, absolutely gorgeous! Thanks to illustrator, Orrin Lundgren who patiently illustrated, illustrated, and again illustrated the pictures we kept on sending. We were so lucky to have you! Thanks to the proofreader Val Anderson, and cover illustrator Barbara Zaretskey, for without start and finish there would never be a completion. Thanks tremendously to the owners of the locations used during photography : Cathy and Larry Skylar at the Albemarle Inn, Asheville, NC; Beth and Jim Berutich at the Chestnut Inn, Asheville, NC; Marge Dente and Gail Kinney at the Owl's Nest Inn, Candler, NC; Horst Brunner and Giselle Hopke at The Ivivi Lodge, Lake Lure, NC; and Arthur and Zee Campbell at the Spring House farm in Marion, NC. Special thanks to Renee Augins, owner of Yarn Paradise in Asheville, NC, for lending yarn for photography.

We like to thank the following companies for their generous contribution of yarn and materials that have made our afghans more than beautiful: Margery Winters and Deana Gavioli from Berroco Yarns, Peggy Wells from Brown Sheep Company, Kathy Lacher from Classic Elite Yarns, Kathleen Sams from Coats & Clark, Claudia Langmaid and Kristina Good from Colinette Yarns, Susan C. Druding from Crystal Palace Yarns, Therese Chynoweth from Dale of Norway, Claudia Castelli from Darice International, Norah Gaughan from JCA/Reynolds Yarns, Nancy Thomas from Lion Brand Yarns, Judith Shangold from Manos del Uruguay, Kristin Muench and Jessica from Muench Yarns, June Bridgewater from Rowan Yarns, Josie Dolan from S.R. Kertzer, and Barry Klein and Heidi Berger from Trendsetter yarns.

Thanks to all the librarians who helped us in our research, especially Deborah Goeff from Greene County Public Library in Xenia, OH, and Julianne Fornell from Detroit Public Library's Main Branch in Detroit, Michigan.

index

An integral part of this book cannot have been accomplished without the support, encouragement of our family and friends: We would like to thank our paternal grandparents, Fazloor Rahman and Jameela Khatoon, whose creativity passed to us. To our maternal grandparents, Bashir Ahmed Khan Sherwani and Haseeba Khatun, who have taught our Mother all that they know. Our heart-filled thanks goes to our uncles Jaffar, Parvez, and Dr. Taher Ahmed Khan Sherwani, who always encouraged us to reach beyond ourselves. To our aunts, Tahera, Abeda, Rasheda, and Shaheda whose love and handicrafts are still alive to be remembered. To Mohammad Alam and Abdullah whose patience, caring and support helped bring our work to a completion. Thanks to our cousins Amir, Amera, Rizwana, Farrid, Rashed, Zainab, Saadeya, Nabeela, Sabahat, Zahed, Haseeb, Farhan, Tayyiba, Fayyadh, Akmam, Haseeba, Shuaib and Saad for their love, enthusiasm, and support. Our gratitude goes to dearest Fatimah Muhammad (chi hi) and Muhammad Abdur Raheem, whose constant support cannot be forgotten. To sweet "Aisha Aunty" who has always been proud of our achievements. To our friend Fatimah Mehtar whose love for crafts matches our own. Special thanks go to Mrs. Mehtar, Maulana Mehtar and family for their advice and support. Last but not least, to Aunty Maimoona, Uncle Iqbal Bholat, Aunty Bilqees and Uncle Arif Abdul-Majid who have never been surprised at our accomplishments.

Era on page 41 was first published in KnitNet *Fourth Year Second Edition as Gable Lace.*